81-279

LB3425
.G7
T36
1978

Tanner, James Mourilan
Education and physical
growth.

DUE		
MAY 08		
NOV 06		

EDUCATION AND PHYSICAL GROWTH

EDUCATION AND
PHYSICAL GROWTH

*Implications of the study of children's growth
for educational theory and practice*

J.M. TANNER, MD, DSc, FRCP

*Professor of Child Health and Growth,
Institute of Child Health, University of London
Honorary Consultant Physician,
The Hospitals for Sick Children,
Great Ormond Street, London*

Second Edition

INTERNATIONAL UNIVERSITIES PRESS, INC.
NEW YORK

Library of Congress Cataloging in Publication Data

Tanner, James Mourilyan
    Education and physical growth.

    Bibliography: p.
    Includes index.
      1.   Children in Great Britain—Anthropometry.
2. Children—Growth.   3. Education of children.
4. Child development.   I. Title.
LB3425.G7T36   1978   573'.6   78–8809
ISBN 0-8236-1531-6

ISBN 0-8236-1531-6
First published 1961
Second edition 1978

Printed in Great Britain
by J.W. Arrowsmith Ltd, Bristol

Preface to the Second Edition

In the fifteen years that have elapsed since the publication of the first edition of this book considerable advances have taken place in our knowledge of physical growth, if not—and I believe the matter is disputed—in education. So far as auxological principles go, nothing much has changed; most of the advance has been in matters of detail. As a result we see more clearly now, for example, the importance of sensitive or critical periods in growth; the manner in which the brain and endocrine glands control the initiation of puberty; the relative importance of nutritional and social stimulation in the early development of the nervous system; the extraordinary resilience of the young organism in its ability to recover through 'catch-up' growth. We have been relieved of the never very real fear that the secular trend toward earlier maturity would march on towards the nursery school.

But the lessons we can draw for education from Human Biology remain; and remain, perhaps, to be learned. Has education progressed from the apple-sorter towards the network? Have the implications of biological variability made headway in the minds of the educational planners? Have the sufferings of early and late maturers met a more ready response from the teachers? Those are matters I must ask the reader to decide.

I have revised and up-dated where necessary all parts of the book, and in particular the chapters relating to the development of the brain and the interaction of hereditary and environmental factors in controlling growth. In regard to the latter I have been much helped by the immense compilation and synthesis of data made possible by the recent International Biological Programme and reported in *World-wide Variation in Human Growth* (P.B. Eveleth and J.M. Tanner, Cambridge University Press, 1976).

In one particular respect the first edition of this book proved very useful to its author. From 1963 to 1966 I served on the Plowden Committee on Primary Education (*Children and their Primary Schools*, Vols I, II, a Report of the Central Advisory Council for Education; Her Majesty's Stationery Office, 1967). The experience was wholly enjoyable and rewarding and I emerged with enhanced liking as well as respect not only for my colleagues on the Committee (whose desire actually to help children and not necessarily administrators burned bright and clear throughout the whole period) but for the educational profession as a whole. We visited scores of schools, and sat through dozens of conferences; very seldom indeed did I feel the chill of evaporating idealism. This preface must serve as a belated thank-you to all my friends and acquaintances of that time.

As before, I would like to acknowledge the good fortune of my post at the Institute of Child Health and The Hospitals for Sick Children, Great Ormond Street, and as well the financial support of the Nuffield Foundation whose faith established my department as a going concern over the last fifteen years, when government money was conspicuous by its absence. Also as before, I wish to thank my colleague Mr R.H. Whitehouse for again making the charts, correcting the proofs and pointing out much in the study of growth that I would otherwise be unaware of; my wife Dr B.A. Tanner for numerous discussions, not all officially about education; and Miss Janet Baines and Miss Sara Dunford for preparing the manuscript.

London, August 1976   J.M. Tanner

Preface to the First Edition

This book is addressed to teachers, to lecturers in colleges, institutes and university departments of education, and to all those whose professional or personal interests make them concerned with our educational system. The aims and the contents of the book are outlined in the first few pages of Chapter 1. I have tried to present in a form suitable for teachers the salient facts concerning the physical growth of children, and those principles derived from them which seem to me to have a direct bearing on educational practice. Such, for example, is the notion of developmental or physiological age, derived from the greatly differing rates of physical maturing seen in children. Such, also, is the idea of the growth gradient, derived from the occurrence of set orders in which parts of the body, including the brain, approach maturity.

We know lamentably little about the growth and development of the brain in children, but I have made a special effort to present what little information exists, for the importance of such knowledge to teachers needs no emphasis. Readers without some biology in their educational background may find this chapter difficult, but I hope not impossible, going; some parts are less technical than others, as judicious skipping will show. The most technical passages have been relegated to footnotes.

I have discussed the occurrence of stages of growth and of critical periods of development, since they are subjects much written about by educationists and psychologists. The current trend toward greater size and earlier maturing has been also much discussed recently and I have supplied the figures which form the basis of this discussion. Both environmental and genetical explanations for the earlier maturing have been put forward and I have given a full, though elementary, description of the effects on growth of various factors, such as nutrition, health, psychological influences, socio-economic class and family size, in discussing generally the interaction of heredity and environment in controlling the growth process.

Throughout the book, and especially in the final chapter, I have indicated some of the consequences of the facts of physical growth and development for education; but teachers themselves are the persons best fitted to appreciate the full implications of these facts and viewpoints, and in doing so I hope they will find that this knowledge proves useful in their everyday practice.

The book originated in a series of lectures given at the University of Leeds Institute of Education in June 1960. I am most grateful to all the members of the Institute for their hospitality, and I particularly wish to thank Dr K. Lovell, at whose suggestion the lectures were undertaken, Miss F.M. Stevens for working through the manuscript with her teacher-students, and all those who attended the course and provided after each lecture a prolonged barrage of thought and opinion. I am grateful also to Miss M. Brearley and her staff at the Froebel Education Institute, Mr S. Redman of the Oxford University Institute of Education, and my wife, Dr B.A. Tanner, for making most helpful observations on the manuscript. I wish to acknowledge most warmly all the support the Institute of Child Health has given me over the last few years, and particularly the help and encouragement of Professor A. Moncrieff, its Director. I wish also to thank my assistant, Mr R.H. Whitehouse, for making the charts, and many of the calculations upon which they are based, and my secretary, Miss Shirley Jarman, for preparing the manuscript and assembling the bibliography.

Finally, I am very conscious that, despite the best efforts of my educationist friends, there may remain in these lectures mistakes of selection and misjudgements of emphasis. I can only appeal to my readers to help me in removing gaps, ambiguities and inconsistencies by pointing them out to me. Should a second edition then be called for I might hope to make the book more useful to the teachers and instructors to whom it is particularly addressed.

London, December 1960   J.M. Tanner

Contents

1   Introduction and Synopsis   11

2   The Course of Children's Growth   15
The growth curve of height. Types of growth data. Growth curves of different tissues and different parts of the body. Growth and development at adolescence. Endocrinology of growth. Development of the reproductive system.

3   Developmental Age and the Relation between Physiological and Mental Maturity   34
Skeletal age. Dental age. Relations between different measures of maturity. Sex differences in developmental age. Physical maturation and mental ability. Physical maturation and emotional development.

4   Organization of the Growth Process   50
Canalization and catch-up. Competence and specification. Sensitive periods. Growth gradients. Disorganization of growth. Stages of development: general and singular. Prediction of adult size from size in childhood.

5   Growth and Development of the Brain   67
Morphological development. Cerebral cortex development. Hemispheric specialization. Influences on brain development. Physiological development of the brain: the electroencephalogram during growth. Individual differences in brain maturation and the IQ.

6   Interaction of Hereditary and Environmental Factors in Controlling Growth   90
Genetics of size, shape and tempo of growth. Tempo of growth. Differences between races. Climatic and seasonal effects on growth. Nutrition. Illness. Exercise. Psychological disturbance and growth rate. Socio-economic class and numbers in the family.

7   The Secular Trend toward Earlier Maturity   115

8   Implications for Educational Practice and Policy   121
Individual differences in rate of maturing. The question of school-leaving age. Growth and development of the nervous system.

Bibliography   127

Glossary   135

Index   141

CHAPTER ONE

Introduction and Synopsis

The researches of the last fifty years into the physical growth and development of children have led us to a number of general principles governing growth and to a vast array of facts concerning it. It is the contention of this small book that these principles and certain of the more salient facts have implications for educational theory and practice. This is not a novel, and scarcely a disputatious, view; for a long time now we have been trying to relate education more to the nature of the child and less to the convenience of the adult, or even the ultimate demands of the culture. The links between human biology, anthropology and education have always been close, and some of the great educators of the past have come into that field by way of medicine or anthropology.

Experience in lecturing in departments and institutes of education has repeatedly shown me that the majority of teachers have a very lively interest in physical growth, and a strong feeling that behaviour and thinking cannot be considered properly in isolation from body and brain. Indeed many teachers and lecturers in Colleges of Education grasp eagerly at the facts—and sometimes the false rumours of facts—concerning physical development, regarding them as relatively solid straws in the maelstrom of conflicting educational theory.

Not all these facts, however solid, are relevant to education, and in this book I have tried to sort out and present just those facts and those general principles arising from them that seem to me to have a direct bearing on educational practice and planning. Such, for example, are the notions of physical maturity or developmental age, as opposed to chronological age; of growth gradients ensuring the development of different parts of body or brain in a particular order irrespective of whether growth as a whole is accelerated or retarded; of critical periods of growth wherein events must take place or be skipped for ever. Such also are the facts of pubescent development, and of the trend of children towards greater size and earlier physical maturing.

Though this book does not set out to be a text of physical development, certain areas, most notably the growth of the brain, call for something approaching textbook treatment, if only to emphasize what is known and what is not known about them. People working in one field of knowledge repeatedly believe that specialists in another must necessarily have mopped up those pockets of ignorance that are in principle assailable. The medical man is astounded to find a major work of Galen available only in the original Greek or in mediaeval Latin: the historian shrugs his shoulders; there is too much to do. Similarly the educationist and psychologist may be astonished to hear that we know next to nothing about brain growth after 2 years old. In principle no obstacle, at least to anatomical description, exists; a little money and a determination to organize and support research would remove this particular ignorance. But no body exists to support such work; our medical research organizations tackle the problems of disease rather than those of healthy development, and our educational researchers have so far been too busy measuring the mind to consider describing the brain. The pace of our advance in understanding how a child grows is slower than it need be, but nevertheless we do advance and it is upon the advances of the last few years that the thoughts in this book rest.

Chapter 2 presents a general description of growth from birth to maturity, with descriptions of the growth curves for height, other skeletal dimensions, weight, muscle and subcutaneous fat. The acceleration of growth that occurs at adolescence is discussed, together with the changes in physiological function which occur at the time. It is these changes which give rise to most of the characteristic differences between boys and girls in strength and endurance, as well as in the more direct aspects of reproduction.

Different children experience these adolescent changes at very different ages, so that among a group of 14-year-old boys there will be some who have not yet started their adolescent spurt of growth and others who have practically completed it. This variability, which is almost entirely biological in origin, has important social and educational consequences. Though seen most clearly at adolescence, the variability occurs at all ages, some children being advanced and others retarded in physical maturity throughout the whole growing period. To get over this difficulty the concept of physiological maturity or developmental age has been developed and Chapter 3 is devoted to its description, measurement and implications. The question is raised, for example, as to whether physically advanced children are on average also mentally advanced in the sense of being better able to answer intelligence test items, and whether they have a better chance in school examinations than physically retarded children of the same chronological age.

One of the chief methods of measuring developmental age is by the appearance of the bones of the hand or knee. This is because these bones pass through a series of stages of development, recognizable in X-ray photographs. These stages are reached in a particular order, which in general remains unaltered even though the whole development is slowed down, for instance, by starvation. In other words, a *gradient of growth* exists controlling the order in which different parts develop. We see the same in the development of the limbs, where at any time after birth the hand and foot are nearer their adult size than are the forearm and calf. These gradients are discussed in Chapter 4. They are in principle important for education in that they also occur in the growth of the brain and thus condition the order in which abilities and various sorts of behaviour may be expected to emerge. In Chapter 4 also the occurrence of *critical* or *sensitive periods* of growth is discussed. It is known that in animals periods occur during which a particular stimulus from the environment will evoke a particular behaviour or ability in the animal. Once evoked, the ability may remain for life, but if not evoked during this limited period, the ability never appears. The importance of establishing whether such periods occur in the child, and if they do, of defining their exact nature and limits, is obvious.

It is the occurrence of gradients and sensitive periods in the growth of the brain that is of paramount importance for educators, and so in Chapter 5 a description of our present knowledge of the brain's growth is given. The way in which this information may be related to stages of mental development as described, for example, by the school of Piaget, is still almost entirely speculative, but merits at least a preliminary discussion, and this also appears in Chapter 5.

The resilience of children's growth even under the worst circumstances is very great, though from a biological point of view not at all unexpected. For young animals to survive there must be inherited mechanisms of regulation to keep the animal following faithfully its trajectory of growth, and evolution has seen to it that such mechanisms exist. Thus growth is in general a very regular process, and subject to certain limitations it is possible to predict to a surprising degree an adult's size and shape from his size and shape as a child. This predictability of growth is discussed in Chapter 6, together with the whole interplay of hereditary and environmental forces acting together to control or upset the growth process. The effects of malnutrition and of illness, for example, are briefly outlined.

Children at all ages are nowadays bigger than they were seventy or even thirty years ago. This is partly because they are growing into bigger adults, but also because they are maturing faster; a child of 5 now is in all physical, and probably a good many psychological, respects equivalent to a child of 6 of thirty years ago. This *secular trend* in growth, as it is called, is one of the most striking findings of human biology in recent years, and has very far-reaching effects. It may well explain, for example, why, in the classical Scottish study of the IQs of 11-year-old children in 1932 and 1947, the fall predicted on genetical grounds failed to occur. In fact, not constancy but a small rise due to the secular trend should have been expected, barring these genetical considerations. The secular trend and its results are discussed in Chapter 7.

Finally, in Chapter 8, the implications of the previous chapters for educational policy and practice are brought together and summed up. Chief amongst them is the demand for a social variabilty to match the biological variability of growth rates. Individual differences in maturation, both in speed and manner, cannot be eliminated or even much altered; they can only be met by an educational system of great flexibility, a system based on a network rather than a production line.

CHAPTER TWO

The Course of Children's Growth

The growth curve of height

In Fig. 1 is shown the growth curve in height of a single boy, measured every six months from birth to 18 years. Above is plotted the height attained at successive ages; below, the increments in height from one age to the next. If we think of growth as a form of motion, and the passage of a child along his growth curve as similar to the passage of a train between stations, then the upper curve is one of distance achieved, and the lower curve one of velocity. The velocity, or rate of growth, naturally reflects the child's situation at any given time better than does the distance attained, which depends largely on how much the child has grown in all the preceding years. Accordingly it is usually more important to concentrate on the velocity rather than on the distance curve. In some circumstances the acceleration may reflect physiological events even better than the velocity; thus at adolescence it seems likely that the great increase in secretions from the endocrine glands is manifested most clearly in an acceleration of growth. In general, however, nothing more complex than velocity curves will be considered here.

The record in Fig. 1 is the oldest published study of the growth of a child; it was made during the years 1759 to 1777 by Count Philibert Guéneau de Montbeillard upon his son, and published by Buffon in a supplement to the *Histoire Naturelle*. It shows as well as any more modern data that in general the velocity of growth in height decreases from birth (and actually from about the fourth intrauterine month) onwards, but that this decrease is interrupted shortly before the end of the growth period. At this time, from 13 to 15 in this particular boy, there is a marked acceleration of growth, called the *adolescent growth spurt*. From birth up to age 4 or 5 the rate of growth declines rapidly, but the decline, or deceleration, gets gradually less, so that in some children the velocity is practically constant from 5 or 6 up to the beginning of the adolescent spurt.[1]

---

[1] A slight increase in velocity of height growth from about 6 to 8 years, providing a second wave on the general velocity curve, has sometimes been thought to occur and has been

As the points of Fig. 1 show, growth is an exceedingly regular process. Contrary to opinions still sometimes met, it does *not* proceed in fits and starts. The more carefully the measurements are taken, with, for example, precautions to minimize the decrease in height that occurs during the working day for postural reasons, the more regular does the succession of points on the graph become. In a series of children each measured for seven years or more by the same measurer, my colleagues and I have found that at least over the age range 3 to 10 the deviations of the actual points from a very simple mathematical curve

$$\text{Height} = a + bt + c \log t \quad (\text{where } t \text{ is age})$$

were seldom more than 6 mm, or $\frac{1}{4}$ in., and were on average equally above and below the curve at all ages (see Fig. 2). There is no evidence for 'stages' in height growth except for the spurt associated with adolescence. Perhaps the increments of growth at the cellular level are discontinuous, and proceed by starts and stops; but at the level of bodily measurements, even of single bones measured by X-rays, one can only discern complete continuity, with a velocity that gradually varies from one age to another.

The adolescent spurt is a constant phenomenon, and occurs in all children, though it varies in intensity and duration from one child to another. In boys it takes place, on the average, from $12\frac{1}{2}$ to $15\frac{1}{2}$, and in girls about two years earlier, from $10\frac{1}{2}$ to approximately $13\frac{1}{2}$. The peak height velocity reached averages about 9 cm ($3\frac{1}{2}$ inches) per year in boys and a little less in girls; this is the rate at which the child was growing at

called the juvenile or mid-growth spurt. I can find no satisfactory evidence of its presence in the individual records covering the period 3 to 13 that are known to me.

Some teachers have acquired the quite erroneous notion that growth occurs in a series of alternating periods of 'stretching up' (increased velocity in height) and 'filling out' (increased velocity in breadth). The idea seems to have originated in 1896 in a paper by Winfield Hall, an American school doctor, who measured, very carefully, some 2,400 boys aged 9 to 23. The study was cross-sectional, with between 100 and 300 in each yearly age group. Medians were calculated but no standard deviations. The 13-year-old value for height was rather higher than might have been expected. Though to the modern eye its deviation is well within the limits of sampling error, Hall took it at face value and thus obtained a large 12-13 increment, small 13-14 increment and large 14-15 increment, this last being the adolescent spurt proper. In circumferences of the joints this did not occur, the curves being fairly regular. Hence, when the values were expressed as percentages of the 9-year-old value, the distance curves for height and for circumferences crossed at 12-13, 13-14 and 14-15. Hall thereupon formulated (in italics) a Law of Growth: 'When the vertical dimension of the human body is undergoing an acceleration in its rate of growth the horizontal dimensions undergo a retardation and vice versa'. The idea was taken up and generalized to the whole period of growth by the German anthropologist C. H. Stratz, who in many articles wrote of a first *Streckung* at 5 to 7 and a second at 8 to 10. The data on which these opinions were based were quite insufficient to support them, but somehow they got into textbooks, where in some instances they have remained safely cocooned till the present day, despite the severest attempts to dislodge them by people such as Schiotz (1923) whose measurements of children were adequate in number, taken longitudinally (see below), and interpreted with statistical sense.

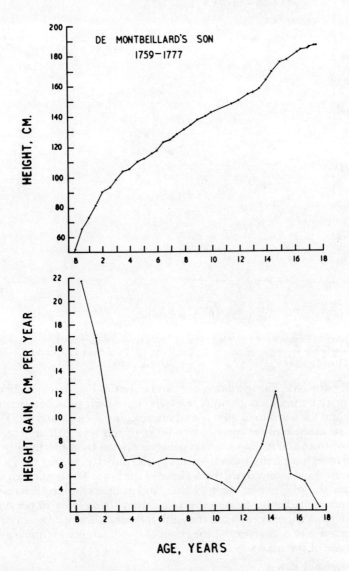

Fig. 1. Growth in height of de Montbeillard's son from birth to 18 years, 1759-77. Above, distance curve, height attained at each age; below, velocity curve, increments in height from year to year. Data from Scammon, 1927, *Amer. J. phys. Anthrop.* (From Tanner, *Growth at Adolescence,* Blackwell: Oxford.)

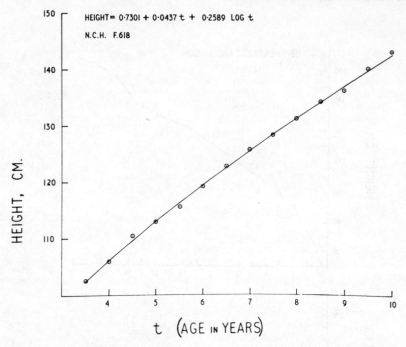

Fig. 2. Curve of form $y = a + bt + c \log t$ fitted to stature measurements taken on a girl by R.H. Whitehouse every six months from age $3\frac{1}{2}$ to 10. Data from Harpenden Growth Study. (From Israelsohn, 1960.)

about 2 years old. The sex difference can be seen in Fig. 3, which shows the velocity curves for a group of boys who have their peak between 14 and 15 and for a group of girls with their peak between 12 and 13. The earlier occurrence of the spurt in girls is the reason why girls are bigger than boys from about $10\frac{1}{2}$ to 13 years. Boys are larger than girls by only 1-3 per cent in most body measurements before puberty, so that the girls' adolescent spurt soon carries them ahead of the boys. The boys catch up and pass the girls when their greater and probably more sustained adolescent spurt begins to take effect, and they finish some 10 per cent larger in most dimensions. Thus the adult difference in size between men and women is to a large extent the result of the difference in timing and magnitude of the adolescent spurt.

Types of growth data

In Fig. 1 the measurements of a single individual child were plotted and not averages derived from different children each measured at a different age. The distinction is important, for the two approaches do not give the same curve. The method of study using the same child at each age is called *longitudinal*; that using different children at each age, *cross-sectional*. In a cross-sectional study each child is measured once only, and all the

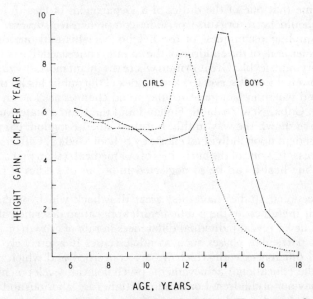

Fig. 3. Adolescent spurt in height growth for girls and boys. The curves are from subjects who have their peak velocities during the modal years 12-13 for girls, and 14-15 for boys. Actual mean increments, each plotted at centre of its half-year period. Data from Shuttleworth, 1939, Tables 23 and 32. (From Tanner, *Growth at Adolescence*, Blackwell: Oxford.)

children at age 8, for example, are different from all those at age 7. In a longitudinal study, on the other hand, each child is measured at each age and all the children at age 8 are the same as those at age 7. A study may be longitudinal over any number of years from two upwards. In practice it is always impossible to measure exactly the same group of children every year for a prolonged period; inevitably some children leave the study and others, if that is desired, join it. A study in which this happens is called a *mixed longitudinal* study, and special statistical techniques are needed to get the most out of its data.

Both cross-sectional and longitudinal studies have their uses, but they do not give the same information and cannot be dealt with in the same way. Cross-sectional surveys, like the one the London County Council used to carry out every five years on the children in its schools (see Scott,1961), are obviously cheaper and more quickly done, and can include far larger numbers of children. They tell us much of what we want to know about the distance curve of growth. Thus they are the appropriate method for constructing standards for height and weight attained by healthy children at each age, for use in schools and clinics (e.g. the Tanner-Whitehouse 1959 standards for British children). Such periodic surveys are very valuable, particularly in following the secular trend (see Chapter 7) and the health of the child population as a whole. Indeed it seems to me that one of the duties of a Department of Health in any country should be to organize periodic comprehensive surveys, using proper sampling techniques, of the heights, weights and one or two further dimensions of the children of the country concerned. Particularly is this so in countries like Great Britain where the infant mortality rate has been so lowered that it serves less as an index of the public health than it used to and where in fact great secular trend changes are known to be occurring. Cuba, New Zealand, Holland and the United States, among others, have shown the way in this, but the United Kingdom has so far been dependent upon individual efforts by School Medical Officers in its various areas. It is one of the curiosities of our medical system that a study of the public health can be so neglected in favour of studies of public disease.

Cross-sectional studies have one great drawback which practically limits their usefulness to the public health application described above. They can never reveal individual differences in rate of growth or in the timing of particular phases such as adolescense. It is precisely these individual differences with which we are concerned and which throw light on the educational achievement, psychological development and social behaviour of children. Longitudinal studies are laborious and time-consuming; they demand great perseverance and patience on the part of those who make them and those who take part in them; and they demand very high technical standards, since in the calculation of a growth rate from one age to another two errors of measurement occur, one at each of the ages. Nevertheless most of our knowledge of child growth comes from the few longitudinal studies that have been carried through. In this field at least the school teacher with ambitions to contribute to knowledge of growth is better placed than most of his medical colleagues; for he has a group of children who will mostly stay with him over a considerable period of years.

Cross-sectional data can in some important respects be very mislead-ing. Fig. 4 illustrates the effect on 'average' figures produced by the individual differences in the age at which the adolescent spurt starts. Fig. 4A (left half of Fig. 4) shows a series of individual velocity curves from 6 to 18 years, each individual starting his spurt at a different time. The average of these curves, obtained simply by treating the values cross-sectionally and adding them up at ages 6, 7, 8, etc., and dividing by five, is shown by the heavy interrupted line. It is obvious that the line in no way characterizes the 'average' velocity curve; on the contrary, it is a complete travesty of it. It smooths out the adolescent spurt, spreading it along the time axis. Averages at each age computed from cross-sectional studies inevitably do this and resemble the interrupted line; they fail to make clear the speed and intensity of the individual spurt. In Fig. 4B (on the right) the same curves have been arranged so that their points of maximum velocity coincide; here the average curve characterizes the group quite nicely. In passing from 4A to 4B the time-scale has been

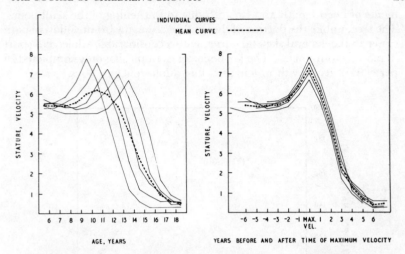

Fig 4. Relation between individual and mean velocities during the adolescent spurt. In Fig. 4A, left, the height curves are plotted against chronological age; in Fig. 4B, right, they are plotted according to their time of maximum velocity. After Shuttleworth, 1937. (From Tanner, *Growth at Adolescence*, Blackwell: Oxford.)

altered, in fact, so that in 4B the curves are plotted not against chronological age, but against a measure which arranges the children according to how far they have travelled along their course of development, in other words, according to their true developmental or physiological status. We shall return to consider this point at length in Chapter 3.

Growth curves of different tissues and different parts of the body

Most measurements of the body show a growth curve generally similar to the curve of height given in Fig. 1. The great majority of skeletal and muscular dimensions, whether of length or breadth, grow in this manner. But some exceptions exist, most notably the brain and skull, the reproductive organs, the lymphoid tissue of the tonsils, adenoids and intestines, and the subcutaneous fat. Fig. 5 shows these differences in diagram form, using size attained, or distance curves. Height follows the 'general' curve. The reproductive organs, internal and external, follow a curve which is not, perhaps, very different in principle, but strikingly so in effect. Their prepubescent growth is very slow, and their growth at adolescence very rapid; they are less sensitive than the skeleton to one set of hormones and more sensitive to another.

The brain and skull, together with the eyes and ears, develop earlier than any other part of the body and have thus a characteristic postnatal curve. Brain growth and development is discussed in detail in Chapter 5; suffice it here to say that by 1 year old the brain has attained about 60 per cent of its adult weight, and by 5 years about 90 per cent. Probably it has no adolescent spurt, although a slight spurt does occur in the measurements of head length and breadth due to thickening of the skull bones. The face, unlike the portion of the skull encasing the brain, follows a path closer to the general skeletal curve, with a considerable adolescent spurt in most measurements. The jawbone, for example, has only completed 75 per cent of its growth in length before adolescence in boys.

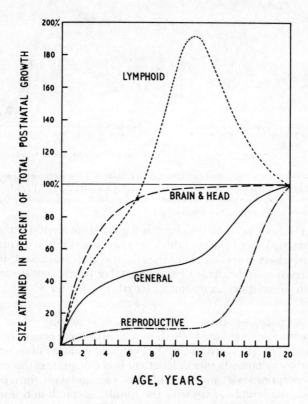

Fig. 5. Growth curves of different parts and tissues of the body, showing the four chief types. All the curves are of size attained (in per cent of the total gain from birth to maturity) and plotted so that size at age 20 is 100 on the vertical scale. Redrawn from Scammon, 1930, *The Measurement of Man*, Univ. Minn. Press. (From Tanner, *Growth at Adolescence*, Blackwell: Oxford.)

Lymphoid type: thymus, lymph nodes, intestinal lymph masses.
Brain and head type: brain and its parts, dura, spinal cord, optic apparatus, head dimensions.
General type: body as a whole, external dimensions (except head), respiratory and digestive organs, kidneys, aortic and pulmonary trunks, musculature, blood volume.
Reproductive type: testis, ovary, epididymis, prostate, seminal vesicles, Fallopian tubes.

The eye seems probably to have a slight adolescent acceleration in growth, though no data are accurate enough to make the matter certain. Very likely it is this that is responsible for the increase in frequency of short-sightedness in children at the time of puberty. Though the degree of

myopia increases continuously from at least age 6 to maturity, a particularly rapid rate of change occurs at about 11 to 12 in girls and 13 to 14 in
boys, and this would be expected if there was a rather greater spurt in the
axial dimension of the eye than in its vertical dimension.

The lymphoid tissue has quite a different curve from the rest: it reaches
its maximum value by the beginning of adolescence and thereafter
actually decreases in amount, largely under the influence of the sex
hormones. Accordingly, children with troublesomely large, but otherwise
normal, tonsils and adenoids may generally be expected to lose their
snuffles when adolescence starts.

The subcutaneous fat undergoes a slightly more complicated evolution. Its thickness can be measured either by X-rays, or more simply at
certain sites by picking up a fold of skin and fat between the thumb and
forefinger and measuring the thickness of the fold with a special, constant-
pressure, caliper. In Fig. 6 the distance curves for two measurements of
subcutaneous fat are shown, one taken at the back of the upper arm
(triceps), the other at the back of the chest, just below the bottom of the
shoulder blade (subscapular). The thickness of subcutaneous fat increases
from birth to reach a peak at nine months or a year, and thereafter
decreases, rapidly at first and then more slowly, until about 6 to 8 years,
depending on the individual child. At that time the width of fat begins to
increase again. In the trunk fat (subscapular measurement) this increase
continues up to maturity in both boys and girls. The limb fat (triceps
measurement) follows this same pattern in girls, but in boys it thins out at
the time of the adolescent spurt in height.

The curves for muscle and bone widths follow the general height curve.
Because weight represents a mixture of these various components of the
body its curve of growth is somewhat different from those discussed above,
and often less informative. Though to some extent useful in following the
health of a child, weight has severe limitations; an increase may be due to
bone or muscle or merely to fat. A boy may cease growth in height and
muscle and put on fat instead (as happens in certain clinical circumstances when large doses of cortisone are given) and his weight curve may
continue to look perfectly normal. Even failure to gain weight or actual
loss of weight in an older child may signify little except a better attention
to diet and exercise, whereas failure to gain height or muscle would call
for immediate investigation. For these reasons regular measurements of
height and weight in the schools should be supplemented by measurements of subcutaneous fat by skinfolds, and muscular dimensions by
circumference of upper arm and calf corrected for the covering subcutaneous fat.

Growth and development at adolescence

Practically all skeletal and muscular dimensions take part in the
adolescent spurt. There is a fairly regular order in which the dimensions
accelerate; leg length as a rule reaches its peak first, followed a few months

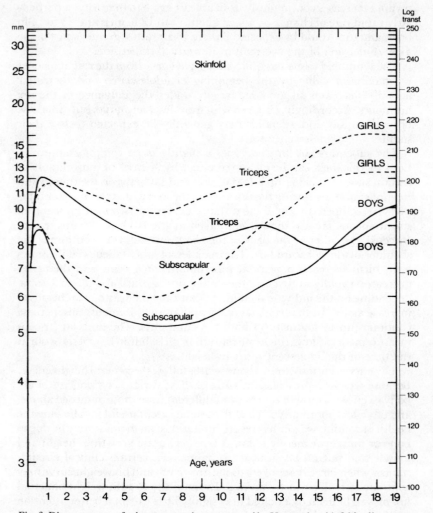

Fig. 6. Distance curve of subcutaneous tissue measured by Harpenden skinfold calipers over triceps (back of upper arm) and under scapula (shoulder blade). Scale is millimetres on the left and logarithmic transform units on the right-hand side. British children, fiftieth centiles. (From Tanner and Whitehouse, 1975, *Archives of Disease in Childhood*.)

later by the body breadths and a year later by trunk length. Most of the spurt in height is due to trunk growth rather than growth of the legs. The muscles appear to have their spurt a little after the last skeletal peak.

At adolescence a marked increase in athletic ability occurs, particularly in boys. The heart, just like any other muscle, grows more rapidly, as can be seen from Fig. 7. The strength of the muscles also increases sharply, especially in boys. The results of two strength tests given to a group of girls

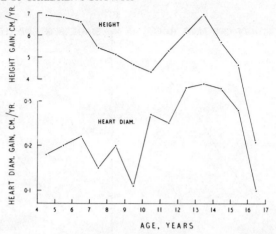

Fig. 7. Velocity curves of transverse diameter of the heart, measured by X-ray, for 71 boys. Mixed longitudinal data, reported cross-sectionally. Height curves of same boys given above for comparison. Data from Maresh, 1948. (From Tanner, *Growth at Adolescence*, Blackwell: Oxford.)

and boys every six months throughout adolescence are plotted (as distance curves) in Fig. 8. Arm pull refers to the movement of pulling apart clasped hands held up in front of the chest, the hands each grasping a dynamometer handle; arm thrust refers to the reverse movement, of pushing the hands together. Each individual test represents the best of three trials made in competition against a classmate of similar ability, and against the individual's own figure of six months before. Only with such precautions can reliable maximal values be obtained. There is a considerable adolescent spurt visible in all four of the boys' curves from about age 13 to 16 (the curves turn more sharply upwards), and a less definite spurt from about 12 to $13\frac{1}{2}$ in the girls' hand-grip curves. There is no sex difference before puberty in strength of arm thrust and little in arm pull (the same is true of calf and thigh muscle strengths). The boys' later superiority arises partly from their greater adolescent growth in muscular bulk, and perhaps partly because the male sex hormone secreted then for the first time may act on muscle to produce more strength per cross-sectional area.

In hand-grip a more considerable sex difference appears to be present as early as age 11. This is a reflection of the greater development, even before puberty, of the male forearm. It is often forgotten that a number of sex differences, besides those of the reproductive organs, antedate puberty, and are not the result of the endocrine gland secretions of adolescence. At birth boys have longer and thicker forearms, relative to upper arms, legs and other parts of the body, and the sex difference increases steadily throughout the whole growing period. (This is not

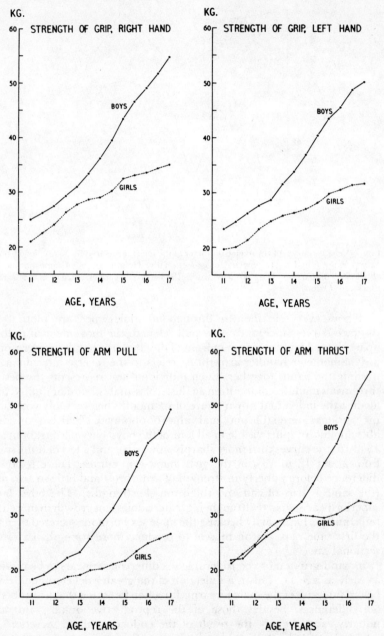

Fig. 8. Strength of hand grip, arm pull and arm thrust from age 11 to 17. Mixed longitudinal data, 65-93 boys and 66-93 girls in each age group. Data from Jones, 1949, Tables 15-22. (From Tanner, *Growth at Adolescence,* Blackwell: Oxford.)

peculiar to man, but occurs in several species of apes and monkeys as well.) Another difference which is already present at birth is the greater length of the second finger in comparison to the fourth in girls. Whether any similar sex differences occur in the brain is not known, but the possibility of them clearly exists (see also Chapters 4 and 5).

Not only the muscles increase in size and strength at adolescence; the vital capacity of the lungs, that is, the amount of air they will hold on maximum inspiration less the amount retained after maximal expiration, also shows a pronounced increase in boys. The number of red blood cells, and hence the amount of haemoglobin in the blood, also rises sharply in boys but not in girls, as shown in Fig. 9. Thus the amount of oxygen which can be carried from the lungs to the tissues increases.

It is as a direct result of these anatomical and physiological changes that athletic ability increases so much in boys at adolescence. The popular notion of a boy 'outgrowing his strength' at this time has little scientific support. It is true that the peak velocity of strength increase occurs six months or a year after the peak velocity of most of the skeletal measurements, so that a short period exists when the adolescent, having completed his skeletal, and probably also muscular, growth, still does not have the strength of a young adult of the same body size and shape. But this is a temporary phase; considered absolutely, power, athletic skill and physical endurance all increase progressively and rapidly throughout adolescence. It is certainly not true that the changes accompanying adolescence even temporarily enfeeble, through any mechanism except a psychological one.

Though the main change at puberty is in body size, there is also a considerable change in body shape. The shape change differs in the two sexes, so that boys acquire the wide shoulders and muscular neck of the man, and girls the relatively wide hips of the woman. Before puberty it is usually impossible to distinguish whether a particular child is a boy or girl from the body proportions or from amounts of bone, muscle and fat alone (despite the few small but perhaps important differences mentioned above). After puberty it is easy to do so in the great majority of cases.

Endocrinology of growth

Thus at adolescence there is a great and sudden increase in body size and strength and a change in many physiological functions beside the reproductive ones. These changes all take place in a co-ordinated manner and a child who is early in respect of one feature is early in respect of all. The changes are mostly more marked in boys than in girls, and take place approximately two years later in boys than in girls.

The immediate cause of all these changes is the secretion into the blood stream (and hence the contact with all tissues) of hormones from the ovaries, testes and adrenal glands. However, ovaries, testes and the particular part of the adrenal which secretes androgenic (i.e. male-determining) hormones have first to be stimulated to grow and function

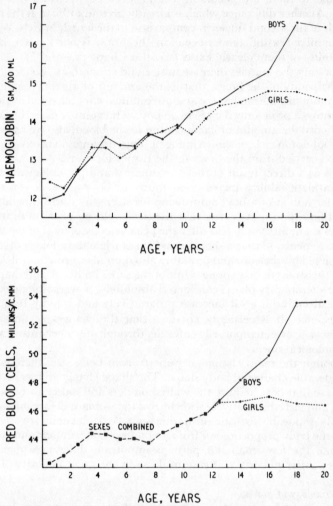

Fig. 9. Change in blood haemoglobin and number of circulating red blood cells during childhood, showing the development of the sex difference at adolescence. Distance curves. Mixed longitudinal data reported cross-sectionally. Redrawn from Mugrage and Andresen, 1936, 1938, *Amer. J. Dis. Child.* (From Tanner, *Growth at Adolescence,* Blackwell: Oxford.)

by other hormones. These come from the pituitary gland, which lies just underneath the base of the brain in approximately the geometrical centre of the head. The pituitary hormones stimulating ovaries and testes are called *gonadotrophins* (gonad being a word which designates both testis and ovary). When the testis is stimulated it secretes *testosterone,* the male sex hormone, and when the ovary is stimulated it produces *oestrogens*, female sex hormones, of which the chief is *oestradiol*.

The pituitary itself, however, awaits the receipt of a chemical stimulus before manufacturing and releasing gonadotrophins and this stimulus comes from a particular small area in the basal part of the brain known as the hypothalamus. This part of the brain lies only just above the pituitary, and its *releasing hormones*, as they are called, are secreted from the tips of nerve fibres and pass to the pituitary by way of a special local arrangement of blood vessels.

The control of the system is a classical example of a simple feed-back. The level of hormone in the blood is like the level of water in the domestic water-tank; when the water reaches a certain mark, the float operates a switch which turns off the pump bringing water to the tank. The feed-back circuit is already operative before puberty. Taking the girls as an example, there is a low level of oestrogen in the blood in childhood, secreted by the ovaries. This level is sufficient to turn off the secretion of gonadotrophin-releasing hormone by the hypothalamus. If the level falls, then releasing hormone is secreted, gonadotrophins produced, oestrogen secretion stimulated and oestrogen blood levels restored. The circuit remains stable in this way till puberty. Then something happens to turn down the sensitivity of the cells in the hypothalamus which sense the oestrogen level. The oestrogen level fails to turn off releaser, releaser rises, gonadotrophin rises, oestrogen rises. Eventually, at a much higher level of oestrogen—a level sufficient to stimulate growth of the breasts and the uterus—the circuit is re-established. In the male the same takes place, with testosterone in place of oestrogen. Just what it is that turns down the sensitivity of the brain cells and thus initiates the whole change, we do not know. It seems probably to be nerve impulses coming from other parts of the brain. Normally this occurs at the end of a long chain of maturational events. Starvation retards puberty, which simply waits for the body to reach its usual pre-pubertal size, irrespective of the passage of time. Maturation of the hypothalamus occurs at a certain moment in the sequence of events, and not, fundamentally, at a certain chronological age. We shall return to this very important point again in the next two chapters.

Sometimes the mechanism goes wrong. There is a hereditary disorder, manifested only in boys, in which a precocious puberty occurs any time from 4 years onwards. When this happens all the events of puberty take place normally, including the production of sperm. In girls a similar, though not hereditary, condition occurs occasionally, and the youngest known mother, who had a child by Caesarian section at age 5, was an example of this. In these cases no other untoward effects take place; the children otherwise are quite healthy. In certain progressive diseases of the brain, however, the hypothalamus may be disturbed and precocious puberty may also occur then.

The factors controlling growth before adolescence are imperfectly understood, but it is clear that another pituitary hormone called *growth hormone* is essential for normal growth to occur. Children who have a deficiency of growth hormone are normal-sized at birth, but grow very slowly thereafter and by two years old have usually fallen below the normal levels for length or height. If untreated they end up as very small adults, of normal proportions and facial appearance, sometimes called miniatures. One of the great recent advances in paediatrics has been the successful treatment of this disorder by means of growth hormone obtained from corpses at autopsy (for animal growth hormone is without effect in man, and the molecule is too large to be synthetized). Treatment has to be continued throughout childhood and adolescence; provided the child is diagnosed and treated early, normal stature is nearly always achieved (Tanner, 1975). The early diagnosis of this disorder is one of several reasons for screening the height of children at entry to primary school; measurement of weight by itself is insufficient since the children are fat as well as short.

Several other hormones, notably that secreted by the thyroid gland, have to be maintained within normal limits for growth to occur normally; but they do not act directly to regulate growth rate. Presumably because of the different hormonal control, there is a considerable degree of independence between growth before, and growth at, adolescence.

Development of the reproductive system

The adolescent spurt in skeletal and muscular dimensions is closely related to the great development of the reproductive system which takes place at that time. The sequence of events for the average boy and girl is shown diagrammatically in Fig. 10. This sequence is not exactly the same for every boy and girl, but it varies much less than the time at which the events occur.

The first sign of impending puberty in boys is usually an acceleration of the growth of testes and scrotum (beginning of bar marked 'testis' in Fig. 10). Slight growth of the pubic hair begins a little later, but proceeds slowly until the advent of the general spurt. The accelerations in height and in penis growth begin about a year after the testicular acceleration, when the Leydig cells of the testis have grown and begun to secrete male sex hormone. Axillary hair usually first appears about two years after the beginning of pubic hair growth, though the relationship is sufficiently variable for a very few children's axillary hair to appear first. Facial hair in boys begins to grow at about the same time as axillary hair. There is first an increase in length and pigmentation of hairs at the corners of the upper lip, then a spread of this to complete the moustache, then the appearance of hair on the upper part of the cheeks and just below the lower lip and finally along the sides and border of the chin. This last development seldom occurs until genital and pubic hair development is far advanced. The enlargement of the larynx occurs a little after the spurt in height and the voice begins to deepen perceptibly during the period when the development of the penis is approaching completion. A few boys undergo a slight breast enlargement at puberty, which in the majority is

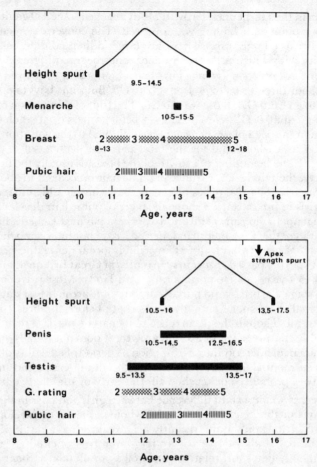

Fig. 10. Diagram of sequence of events at puberty in boys and girls. Average children are represented: the range of ages within which each event charted may begin and end is given by the figures placed below its start and finish. (From Marshall, W.A., and Tanner, J.M. (1970), *Archives of Disease in Childhood*.)

temporary, and soon disappears; only a minority need medical treatment.

In clinical work some designation of how far a child has progressed through puberty is often required, and rating scales have been developed for successive steps of growth of the penis and scrotum in boys, breasts in girls, and pubic hair in both sexes. The scales in each instance range from 1 (prepubescent) to 5 (adult). The numerals in Fig. 10 each refer to the first appearance of the stage in question. Details and illustrations of the stages will be found in Marshall and Tanner (1969, 1970). Genitalia and pubic hair do not necessarily develop in parallel; indeed, some 15 per cent of boys in the Harpenden Growth Study reached stage 4 of genitalia (G4) without pubic hair having yet appeared. The converse sequence, however, is exceedingly rare. There are large individual differences in the rapidity with which a given sequence, once begun, progresses to maturity. For example, on average boys take about a year to go from G2 to G3 and about three years to go from G2 to G5. But some boys take only two years to go from G2 all the way to G5. Thus out of a collection of boys all starting equal at G2 a few reach G5 before others even reach G3. This variation in speed of development is additional to the variation in age of puberty as a whole, and for the most part independent of it.

In girls the beginning of growth of the breast is usually the first sign of puberty, though the appearance of pubic hair precedes it in about 30 per cent of girls. The two series of events show considerable independence: thus girls in breast stage 3 show all stages of pubic hair development, 25 per cent not having any at all and 10 per cent having reached adult status. Menarche, the first menstrual period, is a landmark much used by students of growth and almost invariably occurs after the peak of the height spurt is passed. It occurs currently in Great Britain at an average age of 13.1 years, with a normal range of 10 to 16. Most girls at menarche are in stage 4 of breast and pubic hair, but some are in breast stage 3 and a very small percentage actually menstruate before the breast begins to grow at all. Though the occurrence of menarche marks a definitive and probably mature stage of uterine growth, it does not usually signify the attainment of full reproductive function. A period of infertility of a year or eighteen months follows in most, though not all, cases; and maximum fertility is probably not reached till the early or middle twenties.

There is an important difference between girls and boys in the relative positions of the height spurt in the whole sequence of development at puberty. It has only quite recently been realized, as a result of detailed longitudinal studies on relatively large numbers of children, that girls have their height spurt relatively, as well as absolutely, earlier than boys. The difference between the ages of peak height velocity in girls and boys is just two years, but the difference in the first appearance of pubic hair is about nine months. The first appearance of breasts precedes the first change in testis size by even less. Thus the adolescent growth spurt in girls is placed earlier in the sequence than in boys. Indeed in some girls peak height velocity is reached soon after breast stage 2 and occasionally even before it. Thus for girls the first event of puberty is often an increase of growth velocity, seldom noticed. In boys, on the other hand, the peak height velocity practically never occurs before stage 4 in genitalia growth is reached and it is never the first sign of puberty. This has practical importance, for boys who are late maturers can be reassured that their height spurt is yet to come if genital development is not far advanced; on the contrary, girls who worry about being too tall can be reassured their height spurt is nearly over if menarche has occurred. On average girls grow about 6 cm (roughly 2 in.) after menarche, although gains up to twice this amount may occur. The post-menarcheal gain is practically independent of whether menarche itself occurs early or late.

As in boys, some girls pass rapidly through all stages of breast or pubic hair development while others dawdle. On average the time taken from first appearance of breast bud to reach stage 3 is one year and to reach the adult stage is four years. Girls in rapid transit, however, take only 1½ years to pass through all the stages while dawdlers take as much as five years or even more.

In Fig. 10 the average age of occurrence of each event is given by the scale of age at the bottom on the diagram (e.g. menarche a little after thirteen years). The range of ages within which some of the events may normally occur is given by the figures placed directly below the event (e.g. for menarche 10–16½). A glance will suffice to show how very large these ranges are. One boy, for example, may complete his penis growth at 13½, while another has not even started at 14½. An early maturing boy may have finished his entire adolescence before a late-maturing boy of the same chronological age has even begun his first enlargement of the testes. This ineluctable fact of biology raises difficult social and educational problems, and is itself a contributory factor to the psychological maladjustments often seen in adolescents.

CHAPTER THREE

Developmental Age and the Relation between Physiological and Mental Maturity

Children vary greatly in the age at which they reach adolescence. From a file of photographs of normally developing boys aged exactly 14 it is easy to select three examples which illustrate this. One boy is small, with childish muscles, and no development of reproductive organs or body hair; he could easily be mistaken for a 12-year-old. Another is practically a grown man, with broad shoulders, strong muscles, adult genitalia, and a bass voice; he could be mistaken for a 17-year-old. The third boy is in a stage intermediate between these two. It is manifestly ridiculous to consider all three as equally grown up either physically, or, since much behaviour is conditioned at this age by physical status, in their social relations. The three are simply *not* the same age; if we use that word in any but its literal meaning of the number of days elapsed since birth. The statement that a boy is 14 is in most contexts hopelessly vague; all depends, morphologically, physiologically and sociologically, on whether he is pre-adolescent, mid-adolescent or post-adolescent.

Evidently some designation of physical maturity other than chronological age is needed, and in this instance the obvious one would be the degree of development of the reproductive system. But the same differences in *tempo of growth* occur at all ages, though less spectacularly than at adolescence. We have already seen that the average girl has a faster tempo, that is, matures earlier, than the average boy; and this difference extends right back to birth and before, into fetal life. The same is true within a single sex; in general, boys with an early adolescence are boys whose growth to maturity has been advanced at all ages.

Thus we need a measure of *developmental age* or *physiological maturity* applicable throughout the whole period of growth. Three possible measures exist at present: skeletal age, dental age and shape age. The last may be briefly discussed first, as it is not currently a practical proposition. The child changes shape as he grows (his legs get longer relative to his head, for instance: see Chapter 4) and in principle the degree of shape change could be assessed independently of size by some artful combina-

34

tion of body measurements. Finding the proper combination, however, is a mathematically complex and difficult proposition, and at present this is a research area only. It is an urgent research area in that shape age might have some advantages over skeletal and dental age. Half a dozen body measurements are easy enough to take in school: shape age would be even simpler to assess than skeletal age, and it might be more relevant to educational status than the type of maturity measured by dental age (see below).

Skeletal age

By far the most commonly used indicator of physiological maturity is skeletal age, that is, the degree of development of the skeleton as shown by X-rays. Each bone begins as a primary centre of ossification and passes through various stages of enlargement and shaping of the ossified area. In some cases it acquires one or more epiphyses, that is, other centres where ossification begins independently of the main centre, and it finally reaches adult form when these epiphyses fuse with the main body of the bone. All these changes can be easily seen in an X-ray, which distinguishes the ossified area, whose calcium content renders it opaque to the X-rays, from the areas of cartilage where ossification has not yet begun. The sequence of stages through which the various bone centres and epiphyses pass is constant from one person to another and skeletal maturity, or *bone age* as it is often called, is judged from the number of centres present and the stage of development of each.

In theory any or all parts of the skeleton could be used to give an assessment of bone age, but in practice the hand and wrist is the most convenient area and the one generally used. The hand is easily X-rayed without any radiation being delivered to other parts of the body, it requires only a minute dose of X-rays, and it demands only the minimum of X-ray equipment, such as a dental or a portable machine. Also it is an area where there is a large number of bones and epiphyses developing. The left hand is used, placed flat on an X-ray film with the palm down and the tube placed 30 inches above the knuckle of the middle finger.

The figure for skeletal age is derived by comparing the given X-ray with a set of standards (Greulich and Pyle, 1959; Tanner, Whitehouse, Marshall, Healy and Goldstein, 1975). There are two ways in which this may be done. In the older 'atlas' method the given X-ray is matched successively with standards representing age 5, age 6 and so on and the age standard with which it most nearly coincides is recorded. The more recently developed method is to establish a series of standard stages through which each bone passes and to match each bone of the given X-ray with these stages. Each bone is thus given a score, say, 1 to 8, corresponding to the stage reached and the whole X-ray scores a total of so many maturity points, say, 60. This score is then compared with the range of scores of the standard group at the same age and the percentage of normal children with lower scores at that age is read off. If a particular child's score was such that, say, 80 per cent of normal children of his age had lower scores than he, he would be said to be at the 80th centile for skeletal maturity. A skeletal age may also be assigned, this being simply the age at which the given score 60 lies at the 50th centile.

Readers with experience of mental testing will recognize at once the similarity between each of these methods and methods for assigning mental age or IQ. By the nature of the standards the child who (with enormous improbability) maintained his skeletal development exactly equal to that of the average child of the standarizing group at every age would travel up the line A in Fig. 11, with his chronological and skeletal ages always the same. Line B represents a child who at birth is advanced in maturity but whose *rate* of maturation is a little less than average; he thus gradually falls from above to below the diagonal line. C represents a child consistently retarded in skeletal maturity, with about the same centile status of skeletal age throughout his growth (approximately the 3rd centile).[1]

Dental age

Dental age can be obtained by counting the number of teeth erupted, and relating this to standard figures, in much the same way as skeletal age. The deciduous dentition erupts from about 6 months to 2 years and can be used as a measure of physiological maturity during this period. The permanent or second dentition provides a measure from about 6 to 13 years. From 2 to 6 and from 13 onwards little information is obtainable from the teeth by simple counting, but recently new measures of dental maturity have been suggested which use the stages of calcification of teeth as seen in jaw X-rays in just the same way as the skeletal age uses the stages of wrist ossification.

Relations between different measures of maturity

Skeletal maturity is quite closely related to the age at which certain events of puberty occur. Thus the range of chronological age within which menarche may normally fall is about 10 to 16 years, but the range of skeletal age for menarche is only 12 to 14. Evidently the physiological processes controlling progression of skeletal development are intimately linked to those which initiate menarche. The same is not true, however, of initiation of breast growth in girls or genital growth in boys. In the normal

[1] The figure illustrates a difficulty in the skeletal age concept overcome by the use of simple centiles for skeletal maturity. The spread of the distribution of skeletal age increases with chronological age, so that a retardation of a year at age 12—which is entirely within normal limits—means something quite different from a retardation of a year at age 3— where it would be grossly abnormal. The same problem arises in mental tests, for a similar reason. The ratio skeletal age/chronological age, which is analogous to the IQ, would be constant in child A, dropping slowly at first and progressively faster in B, and dropping at a steady rate in C. The centile status of C, however, would be constant. The difficulty is sometimes overcome for IQs by reporting them as 'deviation IQs'. For these the centile status of the child is first ascertained at the age concerned and then this is converted to an IQ by placing the 50th centile at 100 IQ and the 2½th and 97½th at 70 and 130 respectively.

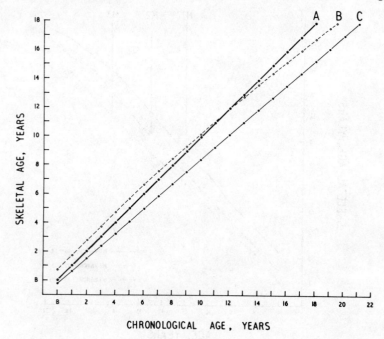

Fig. 11. Skeletal age plotted against chronological age for three hypothetical persons. A, average of standardizing group throughout all growth period; B, initially skeletally mature above average, but passing later to below average; C, consistently below average maturity (a late maturer). (From Tanner, *Growth at Adolescence,* Blackwell: Oxford.)

range of children the time at which these sequences start cannot be usefully predicted from bone age, though in pathological degrees of delay bone age does serve as a useful guide.

As Fig. 12 shows, children tend to be consistently advanced or retarded during their whole growth period, or at any rate after about age 3. Three groups of girls are plotted separately in the figure: those with an early, those with a middling, and those with a late menarche. The early-menarche girls have a skeletal age in advance of the others not only at the time of menarche, but at all ages back to 7; the late-menarche girls have a skeletal age which is consistently retarded. The points M1, M2 and M3 represent the average age of menarche in each group. To be quantitative, the correlation coefficient between age of menarche and skeletal age at 5 or 6 years old, or between age at menarche and percentage of mature height reached then (another measure of maturity), is between 0.5 and 0.6. The correlation becomes less the further back in growth one goes; the children's velocity curves are steeper then and they cross each other more, bringing reassortment of growth status. By and large there is a consistency in acceleration or retardation of skeletal and general bodily maturity.

Dental maturity partly shares in this general skeletal and bodily

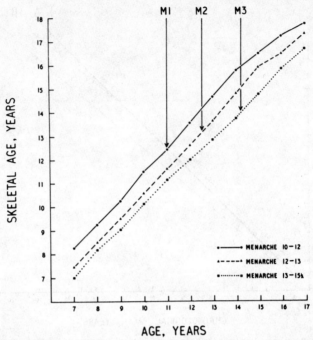

Fig. 12. Relation of skeletal maturity and age at menarche. Skeletal development ages (Todd Standards) for early-, average- and late-menarche groups of girls, from age 7 to maturity. M1, M2, M3, average time of menarche for each group. Mixed longitudinal data. Redrawn from Simmons and Greulich, 1943. (From Tanner, *Growth at Adolescence*, Blackwell: Oxford.)

maturation, and at all ages from 6 to 13 children who are advanced skeletally have on average more erupted teeth than those who are skeletally retarded. Likewise, those who have an early adolescence erupt their teeth earlier, as illustrated in Fig. 13. But this relationship is not a very close one, as the figure also implies: even with only three maturity groups in each sex some crossing of the lines takes place.

This relative independence of teeth and general bodily development is not altogether surprising. The teeth are part of the head end of the organism, and we have already seen in Chapter 1 how the growth of the head is advanced over the rest of the body and how for this reason its curve differs somewhat from the general growth curve. The degree of independence of the teeth should not be over-emphasized, however. In fact, the correlation coefficient between skeletal age and dental age (as measured by the degree of development of the lower third molar tooth as seen in X-rays) for children of the same chronological age in one study was 0.45 (Demisch and Wartmann, 1956).

Evidently there is some general factor of bodily maturity throughout growth, creating a tendency for a child to be advanced or retarded as a

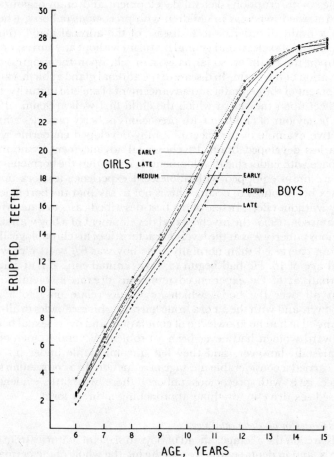

Fig. 13. Total number of erupted teeth at each age for early-, medium- and late-maturing girls and boys. Maturity groups defined by age at peak height velocity. Mixed longitudinal data, reported longitudinally. Redrawn from Shuttleworth, 1939, Table 67 and Fig. 127. (From Tanner, *Growth at Adolescence*, Blackwell: Oxford.)

whole: in his skeletal ossification, in the percentage attained of his eventual size, in his permanent dentition, doubtless in his physiological reactions, probably also in his intelligence test score, as we are about to see, and perhaps in other psychological reactions also. Set under this general tendency are groups of more limited maturities, which vary independently of it and of each other. The teeth constitute two of these limited areas (primary and secondary dentition being largely independent of each other), the ossification centres another, the brain probably several more. Some of the mechanisms behind these relations can be dimly seen: in children who lack adequate thyroid gland secretion, for example, tooth eruption, skeletal development and brain organization are all retarded; whereas in children with precocious puberty, whether due to a brain disorder or to a disease of the adrenal gland, there is advancement of skeletal and genital maturity without any corresponding effect upon the teeth, or, so far as we can tell, upon the progression of organization of the brain. In disease of the adrenal gland at birth, causing development of the genitalia and advancement of skeletal maturity, there is no effect upon the age at which the child first walks (Dennis, 1941).

The behaviour of children with precocious puberty provides a highly instructive example of the effect of a fully developed endocrine system upon a less developed brain. Psychosexual advancement by no means keeps pace with endocrine development. It seems that the hormones need a mature brain equipped with adolescent experience to work upon if adult sex behaviour is to occur. This is not to say that the hormones are entirely without effect. In one of the best-described cases to date (Money and Hampson, 1955) the psychosexual development of a boy with simple precocious puberty was at the level characteristic of his chronological age, but more energized than normally. The boy was $6\frac{1}{2}$ years old, with a skeletal age of 15. He had begun to have seminal emissions at 5 and to masturbate at 6. He experienced numerous dreams involving kissing women all over the body, which he would relate only to a male interviewer, and with the air of a 'roué narrating his escapades in all-male company'. He had no knowledge of copulation, and overt sexual behaviour toward women had never been a problem. Several women on the hospital staff, however, said they felt uncomfortable under his gaze, which carried a considerable message of seduction. In a companion study of three girls with precocious puberty there was little evidence of increased sex drive in anything approaching a direct form.

Sex differences in developmental age

Girls are, on the average, ahead of boys in skeletal maturity from birth onwards, and in dental maturity also during the whole of the permanent dentition eruption (though not, curiously, in primary dentition). It would seem, therefore, that the sex difference lies in the general maturity factor (as well as in various more detailed factors) which prompts the question as to whether it may not exist in intelligence tests and social responses also.

The skeletal age difference begins during fetal life, the male retardation apparently being due to the action of genes located on the Y chromosome, though in what manner we cannot say. At birth boys are about four weeks behind girls in skeletal age, and from then till maturity they remain about 80 per cent of the skeletal age of girls of the same chronological age. It is for this reason that girls reach adolescence and their final mature size some two years before boys. The percentage difference in tooth age is not so great, the boys being about 95 per cent of the dental age of girls of the same chronological age.

Physical maturation and mental ability

We have now reached the principal question of this chapter: to what extent does intellectual and emotional advancement relate to developmental rather than to chronological age? To what extent, if any, does the early developer have a better chance of getting through an age-linked examination, for example? Many authorities make an allowance in examination results for the chronological age of the child, correcting all results back to a standard age of, say, 11.0 years. Should an allowance be made additionally, or instead, for developmental age?

Perhaps the most disturbing aspect of this question is the lack of attention paid to it by educational authorities in this country until recently. For most of the relevant data we have to look elsewhere. These, though not as extensive as one would like, and certainly not as up-to-date, are impressively consistent. As can be seen in the study of the Harvard School of Education, illustrated in Fig. 14, children who are physically advanced for their age do in fact score higher in mental ability tests than those who are less mature, but of the same chronological age. The difference is not great, but it is consistent, and occurs at all ages that have been studied; that is, as far back as 6½ years (Franzblau, 1935; Abernethy, 1936; Freeman and Flory, 1937; Shuttleworth, 1939; Boas, 1941). Similarly, the intelligence test score of postmenarcheal girls is higher than

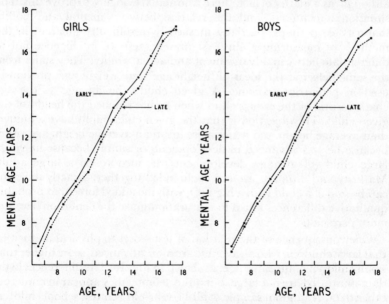

Fig. 14. Growth curves in intelligence test scores for early- and late-maturing boys and girls. Early-maturing boys have peak height velocity before 14½, girls before 12; late-maturing boys after 15½, girls after 13. Mixed longitudinal data, 100-500 subjects in each group at each age. From Shuttleworth, 1939, Tables 14 and 15. (From Tanner, *Growth at Adolescence*, Blackwell: Oxford.)

that of premenarcheal girls of the same age (Stone and Barker, 1937, 1939).

Douglas and his colleagues (Douglas, 1960; Douglas, Ross and Simpson, 1965) have reported similar results for a sample of children drawn from all over Great Britain. Maturity was assessed from degree of secondary sex character development at 14, and it was then found that early maturers had gained significantly more successes in the 11-plus examination than late maturers. Not only were their test papers better; the reports of teachers upon their behaviour in class also favoured them.

The curves in Fig. 14 should be compared with those for tooth eruption in early and late maturers in Fig. 13 and for skeletal development in Fig. 12. It would certainly seem that the brain does share to some small extent in the general factor of bodily maturation during the growing period. The extent, however, is relatively small; the brain is perhaps comparable to the teeth in this respect rather than to the skeleton. Judging by the very old and scanty data available, there is no closer relation between teeth and brain maturities than between either and skeletal maturity.

So far as is known the difference in intelligence test score between early and late maturers vanishes as they complete their growth. By the age of, say, 20 scores of early and late maturers are presumed to be equal, although, as a matter of fact, there is no actual evidence to prove this. The situation is confused, and the relation between mental and bodily maturity is, perhaps, partially masked by a difficulty inherent in the methods of measuring ability. At present, tests of intelligence fail to differentiate between advancement and actual ability. They suffer from the same defect as the ideas of 'height age' and 'weight age' previously used in pediatric medicine. A given child's 'height age' is the age characteristic of the *average* child when he has reached the height of the given child. The objection is that the given child might have a higher-than-average height and hence a greater-than-average height age either because he was advanced in development, or simply because he was a large child (of average development) destined to be a large adult. Maturity and ultimate size are confounded together. Exactly the same can be said of a child with a high IQ, with the added force that probably qualitative differences allied to maturation make the confusion here still more pernicious.

One consequence of the relation of test scores to physical maturity is that large children, who on average are more advanced, score higher than small children of the same age, as shown in Fig. 15. The differences in the data illustrated are not large, but quite definite; they appear in numerous other data. A random sample of all 11-year-old Scottish school children, for example, comprising 6,940 pupils, tested with the Moray House group test, gave a correlation coefficient of 0.25 ± 0.01 between test score and height and 0.19 ± 0.01 between test score and weight when the effect of age on both was allowed for statistically (Scottish Council, 1953). An

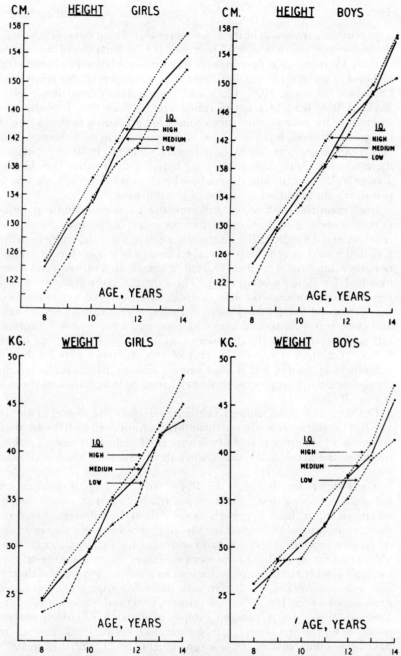

Fig. 15. Curves of height and weight attained at ages 8-14 for boys and girls of high, medium and low intelligence. (IQ, 110 and over, 109-90, below 90.) Cross-sectional data. From Kempf and Collins, 1929. (From Tanner, *Growth at Adolescence*, Blackwell: Oxford.)

approximate conversion of these test scores to Terman-Merrill IQs leads to an average increase of 0.67 points of IQ for each cm of stature, or roughly $1\frac{1}{2}$ points of IQ per inch. A very similar relation has been found in London children (Scott, 1962, table 4). Estimates of this relation in Canadian (Binning, 1958; 1959) and United States data (Boas, 1941; Bayley, 1956) lead to a figure rather greater than this. Probably the strength of the relationship varies somewhat according to the nature of the group studied, but there is no doubt of its general existence. The effects can be very significant for individual children. In 10-year-old girls there was a 9 point difference in IQ between those whose height was above the 75th centile and those whose height was below the 15th. This is two-thirds the standard deviation of the test score.

In all countries students are uniformly the tallest group in the population, averaging 2 to 3 cm taller than the mean of the total population (Eveleth and Tanner, 1976). At the other end of the scale, children in the UK designated as requiring special education in schools for the educationally subnormal were 3 cm less tall at age 11 than others, even when matched for father's occupation. Those in the same National Child Development Survey who were in ordinary schools but whom teachers thought would benefit from such education were about 2.5 cm less tall, and those receiving special help within normal schools were 1.5 cm less tall, again computing the difference within occupational groups of the fathers (Peckham *et al.*, 1977). Part of this difference may be due to differences in tempo, but it is a common finding that mentally handicapped adults are on average smaller than others. Why this should be so is not at all clear.

Children with many siblings (brothers and sisters) are shorter in stature (see p. 113) and score less in tests of ability than children with few siblings. About half the correlation above is associated with differences in sibling numbers; but about half remains when the number of siblings is allowed for.

These differences between the IQs of large and small children are believed to become less as maturity is reached, and to reflect mainly advancement or delay in growth status. Part of the difference, however, may persist into adulthood. It used to be generally taught that in adults no relation existed between IQ and body size, but this seems a questionable statement in the light of modern evidence. There is a quite definite increase in body size from low to high socio-economic groups; and there is also a definite increase in IQ. In such dissimilar groups as conscripted French (Schreider, 1956), Swedish (Husen, 1951) and Norwegian (Udjus, 1964) soldiers, and a random sample of married Aberdeen women pregnant for the first time (Scott, Illsley and Thomson, 1956) correlations have been found between test score and height of 0.29, 0.22, 0.16 and 0.24 respectively. Obviously, such a small correlation is meaningless for the individual. The situation is statistically comparable to accident rates, which do not tell an individual whether he personally will be killed at a particular cross-roads but which nevertheless reflect accurately on the state of the roads at that point.

Whether these relationships reflect genetical or environmental factors is not known; all we can say is that the latter could probably be invoked as a sufficient explanation. It seems likely that differential social mobility also plays a part. It has been shown that in Aberdeen (Thomson, 1959), Belgium (Cliquet, 1968) and France (Schreider, 1964) young persons whose occupation was higher in social status and reward than the occupation of their fathers (the upward socially mobile) were on average taller, as well as brighter, than those who stayed in the same or an equivalent occupation. Fig. 16 illustrates this process in Aberdeen women, both in relation to occupational choice and to later choice of husbands. The subject is extensively reviewed in Tanner (1966).

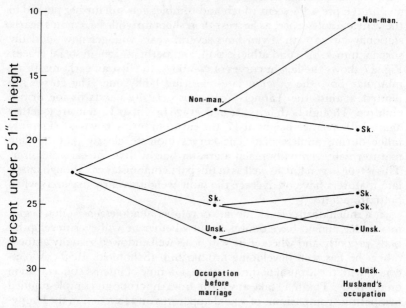

Aberdeen primiparae born to skilled manual workers

Fig. 16. Percentage of daughters, of skilled manual workers, under 5 ft. 1 in. taking non-manual and manual jobs, and marrying men in non-manual, skilled manual and unskilled manual occupations: Aberdeen, 1950s. (Redrawn from Thomson, 1959.)

Physical maturation and emotional development

There is no doubt that being an early or late maturer has repercussions on behaviour, and in some children these repercussions may be consider-able. Though there is little enough solid information on the relation between emotional and physiological development, what there is sup-ports the commonsense notion that emotional attitudes are clearly related to physiological events (Stone and Barker, 1939; Davidson and Gottlieb, 1955).

The world of the small boy is a world of tooth and claw, where physical prowess brings prestige as well as success, and where the body is much more an instrument of the person than in anyone except the athlete in later life. Boys who are advanced in their development, not only at puberty, but before as well, are more likely than others to be the leaders and the top dogs. Indeed, this is reinforced by the fact that muscular, powerful boys on average mature earlier than others and have an earlier adolescent growth spurt. Thus body-build relationships, at least in boys, render even more telling the effects of different tempos of growth. The athletically-built boy not only tends to dominate his fellows before puberty, but by getting an early start he is in a good position to continue that domination. The unathletic lanky boy, unable, perhaps, to hold his own in the pre-adolescent rough and tumble, gets still further pushed to the wall at adolescence, as he sees others shoot up while he remains nearly stationary in growth. Even boys several years younger now suddenly surpass him in size and athletic skill, and perhaps, too, in social graces. Fig. 17 shows the height curves of two boys, the first an early-maturing muscular boy, the other a late-maturing lanky one. The curves are plotted against the Tanner-Whitehouse (1959) standards for British children. Though both boys are of average height at 11, and are together again with average height at 17, the early-maturing boy is considerably taller during adolescence. The curves indicate clearly that the late maturer will eventually reach a greater height than the early maturer. This is true in general, as well as in this particular instance. Though taller, late maturers have on average the same weight as early maturers when both are adult.

At a much deeper level, the late developer at adolescence often begins to wonder and to have doubts about whether he will ever develop his body properly and whether he will be as well endowed sexually as those others he has seen developing around him (Schonfeld, 1950). Adolescence, with the arousal of the sex drive, is a time of intense concentration on the body. This may take any form, from the crude and simple-minded competitive comparisons of sexual apparatus and function in the happy-go-lucky extroverts of residential school or boys' club hut, to the solitary guilt-laden brooding of the sensitive shy boy, afraid to confide his half-realized problems to anyone except, perhaps, an unusually perspicacious family doctor, or an experienced and sympathetic youth leader. Much of the anxiety about sex is, of course, at an unconscious level, and proceeds from sources that are considerably more complex and deep rooted than these. Yet even here the events—or lack of events—of adolescence may act as a trigger to reverberate fears accumulated deep in the mind during the early years of life. The psychoanalysts talk, in rather allegorical language, of the castration complex. By this they mean that there is a certain basic way of reacting to events by being afraid that one's skills, one's 'possessions' in the purely non-material sense, will be taken away from one, or denigrated, and that this way of reacting may be, and in the unconscious mind literally is, symbolized in the act of castration. It needs little imagination to see how these deep-set unconscious fears may be dragged to the surface by an initially superficial and simple anxiety in the sphere of sexual development.

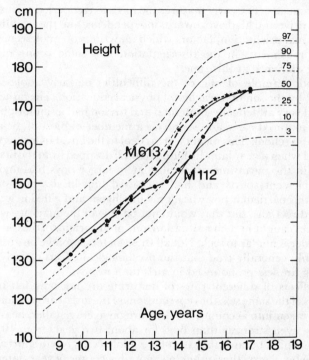

Fig. 17. Height attained from 11 to 17 of two boys of Harpenden Growth Study, one with an early and the other with a later adolescent spurt. The plots are made against the Tanner-Whitehouse British Standards. Note how initially and again finally the two boys are the same height. The early maturer was a very muscular boy, the late maturer a linear boy.

It may seem as though the early maturers have things all their own way. It is indeed true that most studies of the later personalities of children whose growth history is known do show the early maturers as more stable, more sociable, less neurotic and more successful in society, at least in the United States whence all such studies to date have come (Jones and Bayley, 1950; Mussen and Jones, 1957, 1958; Jones, 1957; Jones and Mussen, 1958). Early-maturing girls, in another American study, were considered more grown-up and given higher ratings on social prestige items by their fellow schoolgirls than late maturers of the same age. This was only true, however, in classes composed of girls of about 12 years and older; amongst 11-year-old girls, on the contrary, the higher prestige was accorded to premenstrual girls. Thus both the very early and the very late suffer by comparison with the more average girls (Faust, 1960). The early maturers have their difficulties. Though some glory in their new possessions, others are embarrassed by them. The girl whose breasts are beginning to develop may refuse to stand erect and slouches when asked to recite in front of a class; and the adolescent boy may have similar embarrassments. The early maturer too has a longer period of frustration of his sex drive and his drive towards independence and the establishment of vocational orientation, factors which all writers on adolescence agree are major elements in the disorientation that some young men and women experience at this time.

A good example of one of the difficulties of early adolescence is provided by the son of a teacher of physical education. The father was a short and very athletically-built man and his son had a similar physique. The son matured early and soon was a member of most of the athletic teams in his school. This meant a great deal to the boy. His feelings can be imagined when a year later he found himself dropped from the first teams because in the meantime other ultimately larger boys had undergone their adolescent spurts and had surpassed him in size and strength. Luckily this particular boy was highly intelligent and gifted in a number of other directions. But that would not be true of the majority who find themselves caught in such a situation; one of the origins of the tough little gang leader is not far to seek. Not all these factors impinge on girls, and it is probably generally true that the psychological effects of early or late maturing are less pronounced in girls than in boys.

The effects of different rates of maturing are not only felt between members of the same sex; the repercussions of the girls' earlier adolescence must be taken into account too. Girls are on average taller, heavier and probably even stronger than boys for about two years from $10\frac{1}{2}$ years onwards. This is because they start their adolescent growth spurt at a time when the boys' growth is quite slow; not till a couple of years later do the boys undergo their ultimately more extensive spurt. When boys and girls are educated together we must never lose sight of the fact that girls are physically and emotionally more advanced at all ages than boys.

The ultimate point is that girls are *older*, in any real sense of that term. Eventually we shall have to take cognizance of developmental age rather than chronological age in many fields of education and recreation. It is, for example, highly relevant to the question of school-leaving age. Probably it is good to keep all or most children at school until their adolescense is finished; but if one does this for the late developers that means holding back the early developers in school at a time when some at least of them are straining to get out to productive and practical work. Some solution along the lines of developmental age is easy for the research worker or theoretician to envisage, but difficult for the administrator to apply. The difficulty might not be insuperable, however, if school leaving were more of a graded, and less an absolute, event; if leaving simply implied passage to part-time education or to further part-educational, part-industrial activity. Within a flexible and continuous system, early and late developers would be better able to avoid the present Procrustean Bed, and develop their talents at a tempo and in an environment suited to their individuality.

The assessment of developmental age by medical means, at least in some cases, may be of value to the teacher. An assessment of physical maturity is regarded in many countries as an essential part of the examination of a child referred to the child health service because of behaviour disorders, unexpected educational failure, chronic ill health or sub-standard growth. But the formal determination of physical maturity in a few children is perhaps less important than the general realization amongst teachers of the existence and effects of individual differences in tempo of growth, and the planning of the educational system to accommodate them.

CHAPTER FOUR

Organization of the Growth Process

The growth of the child is a very regular and very organized process. The structure of the adult organism is, for the most part, contained in the extremely small and highly condensed codescript carried in the genes. That is why identical twins, who have identical sets of genes, resemble each other very closely in appearance. They are not, however, *absolutely* the same; on careful measurement and examination some differences in size or shape are nearly always found. These arise because during the long and complex process which intervenes between the primary chemical action of the genes and the finished adult form there are many opportunities for slight deviations, slight discrepancies between chemical reactants, to occur.

For example, when the single fertilized egg divides to give identical twins, it is unlikely that *exactly* equal amounts of cytoplasm go to each half. It is unlikely, therefore, when the chemical substances produced by the genes go out to organize the cytoplasm, that exactly the same concentrations of reactants will be formed in the two developing organisms. As further chemical processes proceed, the opportunity exists for originally small discrepancies to get progressively magnified. Then, as growth continues, the two organisms are affected differently by environment, for their positions in the uterus and their blood supplies are never quite the same. Finally, after birth, even under favourable circumstances of upbringing, the two children are never identical in their total environment, for their food habits are never quite the same, their illness experience never exactly similar.

Canalization and catch-up

The great similarity of identical twins thus requires an explanation, even if their original genes are the same. It is thought, in fact, that the organization of development is such that the processes of differentiation and growth are self-stabilizing or, to take another analogy, 'target-seeking'. The passage of a child along his growth curve can be thought of as analogous to the passage of a missile directed at a distant target. The target is determined by the genetic structure; and just as two missiles may follow slightly different paths but both end by hitting the target, so two children may have slightly different courses of growth but end up with practically the same physique. This self-correcting and goal-seeking capacity was once thought to be a very special property of living things, but now we understand more about the dynamics of complex systems consisting of many interacting substances we realize that it is not, after all, such an exceptional situation. Many complex systems, even of quite simple lifeless substances, show such internal regulation simply as a property consequent on their organization (see Waddington, 1957; Bertalanffy, *Discussions on Child Development, Vol. IV,* p. 155).

This power to stabilize and return to a predetermined growth curve after being pushed, so to speak, off trajectory, persists throughout the whole period of growth and is seen in the response of young animals to illness or starvation. During starvation the animal's growth slows down, but when feeding begins again its velocity increases to above normal, and unless the starvation has been prolonged and severe, the original growth

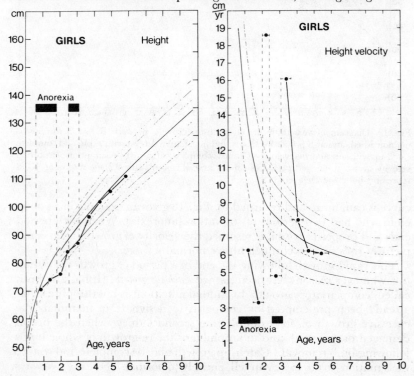

Fig. 18. Height (left) and height velocity (right) in a girl who had two periods of starvation (anorexia).

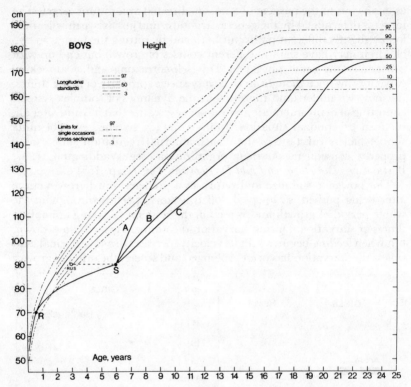

Fig. 19. Diagram of various forms of catch-up growth. Between R and S the boy is malnourished, and at S proper feeding is resumed. Curve A represents rapid and complete catch-up with supranormal velocity, Curve C complete catch-up by resumption of a normal velocity over a prolonged period of time. Curve B is a mixture of these responses. RUS represents bone age, delayed at S.

curve is caught up and returned to. Fig. 18 gives an example in a young child who had two periods of starvation (anorexia). When each period ends and proper nutrition is resumed the velocity of growth (right-hand picture) rises to a level much above normal for age.

This rapid growth following the end of a period of growth restriction (for whatever reason) has been named *catch-up growth*. (It has also been called 'compensatory growth' by animal nutritionists but this phrase has already been pre-empted by zoologists to designate in mammals the excessive growth of, for example, the second kidney, when the first is damaged or removed, and in amphibians the re-growth of whole limbs following limb removal.) Catch-up growth may be complete and restore the situation, so far as we can tell, entirely to normal. There are two ways in which this may be done (Fig. 19). In true complete catch-up the velocity increases to such an extent that the original curve is attained and

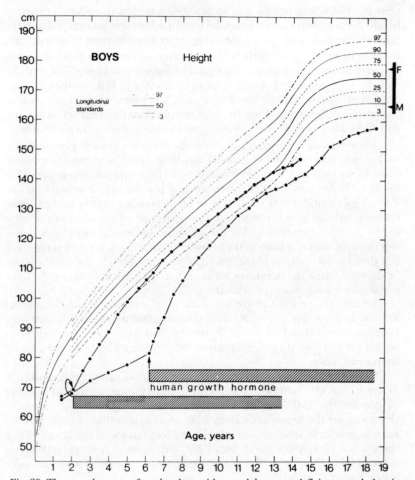

Fig. 20. The growth curves of two brothers with growth hormone deficiency, each showing rapid catch-up when growth hormone is administered. Note that catch-up is more complete in the younger brother, probably because treatment started earlier.

thereafter growth proceeds normally (curve A in Fig. 19). In complete catch-up with delay the catch-up velocity is not sufficient to do this, but maturity is delayed and growth is resumed at the correct velocity for chronological age (curve C) or, usually, for maturity as signified by bone age (curve B). In these cases growth continues for longer, but in the end complete catch-up, or compensation for the growth arrest, is achieved.

Frequently, the catch-up is a mixture of these responses. In Fig. 20 are shown the height curves of two brothers both of whom had isolated growth hormone deficiency from birth. The first, Colin, was not treated till age 6.2 years. By this time, besides being small, he was much delayed in growth, with a bone age of 3.0 'years'. He had a marked catch-up velocity, but it was insufficient to bring him within the normal range of height-for-age curves. However, he remained somewhat delayed and his adolescent spurt took place some eighteen months later than average. Even so he ended just a little below the range of variation expected from his parents' heights (shown in the figure by the vertical barred line with M and F, representing parents' centiles, upon it). His brother, whose treatment started much earlier, at age 2.1 years, showed a classical complete catch-up, reaching the 10th centile after five years of treatment and thereafter continuing along it (notice this is his mother's centile).

Children have an astonishing capacity to return to their growth curve and a five-year-old whose growth has been quite arrested for a whole year, for example by hypothyroidism, will catch up completely provided he is well fed and looked after during his period of rehabilitation. Pathology or undernutrition early in life is another matter and children starved early *in utero* through some imperfection of the placenta usually fail to catch up completely. We do not know for certain why this is so, but it is thought that it relates to the phase of cell multiplication. It seems that cell division has to take place to a tightly organized schedule and cannot be delayed while the organism waits for better conditions, as can the later phase of packing material into the cells.

The actual cause of the greater-than-usual velocity in catch-up is not known. It is not due to greater than normal amounts of growth hormone. Our ignorance about the catch-up mechanism is not too surprising when we reflect that we do not even know why younger animals grow faster than older ones.

One thing does seem to be clear about canalization. Regulation is better in females than in males. This applies to man as well as to other mammals; the radiation of the atomic bombs in Japan, for example, slowed down the growth of exposed boys more than that of girls, and the same is generally true of undernutrition except in social situations where the male is clearly favoured. Similarly, girls recover from growth arrest more quickly than boys. The physiological reason for this greater stability is not known.

We know very little as yet about how these intricate growth patterns are actually organized. The fundamental plan for growth is certainly laid down very early, in the comparative safety of the uterus. For example, an immature bone removed from a fetal or newborn mouse and implanted under the skin of the back of an adult mouse of the same inbred strain (which therefore produces no antibodies to it) will continue to develop until it closely resembles normal adult bone. Furthermore, the cartilage scaffolding of the bone, which is the stage preceding actual bone formation, will do the same if transplanted (Felts, 1959). Thus the structure of the adult bone in all its essentials is implicit in the cartilage model of months before. The later action of the bone's environment, represented by the muscles pulling on it and the joints connecting it to other bones, is limited to the making of finishing touches.

Competence and specification

All cells have a full set of chromosomes and hence of potential assembly lines for all types of protein. But very early in embryological development this general *competence*, as it is called, is lost; each cell concentrates more and more on certain specialized production lines. It seems that the other lines are put into moth balls rather than actually smashed up, but the mothballing is usually pretty thick. Thus when the period of competence of a cell to do something has passed, it is usually impossible to recapture it.

The most thoroughly studied instance is that of the toad retina. There is a small area of the embryonic nervous system which will develop into the neural part of the retina. It is polarized very early into latent front and back ends, as can be shown by taking it out of the body and growing it in tissue culture. However, if it is excised while still an early eye rudiment and replaced back-to-front it is able to change its polarity and a normal eye is formed. The change is made through interaction with the rest of the system surrounding it. However, if the rudiment is excised, left to develop to a more advanced stage outside the body in tissue culture, and then reimplanted back-to-front it can no longer reverse polarity and the eye forms an inverted pattern of nerve connections with the brain. The neurons are now said to be *'specified'* or *'determined'*. Complete specification seems to accompany cessation of the power of dividing. The time at which specification occurs varies from tissue to tissue and even from cell to cell. Specification usually occurs well before any morphological signs are visible: thus experiment reveals certain cells to be specified irreversibly to make a certain part of the brain: but only considerably later can they be identified as actually turning into that part. Specification, in other words, is a matter of molecular form and distribution. The effect of a central nervous system poison in the fetus (for example, thalidomide) depends firstly on the specific chemical affinities of the poison with particular types of cell and secondly on whether these cells and their potential replacements are specified at the time the poison acts.

Sensitive periods

A very important extension of this principle is seen in the concept of *sensitive periods*. These were originally called *critical periods* by biologists and psychologists, and have also, in a more limited context, been referred to as periods of special vulnerability. By a sensitive period is meant a certain stage of limited duration during which a particular influence, from another area of the developing organism, or from the environment, evokes a particular response. The response may be beneficial, indeed perhaps essential for normal development, or it may be pathological.

An example of a sensitive period for a pathological event is well known to everybody. Some children whose mothers have rubella (German measles) between the first and twelfth weeks of pregnancy are born with cataracts in the eyes and other defects. The period of response is strictly limited; it is 'critical' in a very real sense.

To what extent, however, do sensitive periods, periods where a certain normal stimulus must be obtained, occur in healthy development? It seems clear that in the embryo many of the essential linkages in development are of this nature. One of these, at least, we can infer with some confidence. Men and women differ genetically in that the former have one X and one Y chromosome, and the latter two X chromosomes. At approximately the seventh intra-uterine week genes on the Y chromosome, by some series of steps of which we are ignorant, cause the previously undifferentiated reproductive organ tissue to differentiate, and form a testis. This is a critical event, for if it fails to occur then some weeks later the undifferentiated organ differentiates, probably spontaneously, into an ovary. A few children are born with a chromosomal formula XXY; in them the Y gene, outweighed by two Xs, is only partly successful in causing formation of the testis, and sterility results. A second critical period occurs later in the genesis of the male reproductive system. About nine weeks after fertilization, the fetal testis begins to secrete testosterone, and this causes the previously undifferentiated external genitalia to form a penis and scrotum. Once more, if failure to secrete the hormone occurs, then some weeks later the genitalia become, quite passively, definitively female.

A similar period in regard to brain differentiation occurs in many mammals, and in all probability in man also. During the first five days after birth, in the rat, the brain is specially sensitive to testosterone. In the male, this is secreted by the testis and its action renders the brain irreversibly male, so that the endocrine system, which it controls, behaves henceforth in a male, non-cyclic, way. It takes a large dose of testosterone to cause the differentiation during the first two days after birth, a small one on days 3 and 4, and a large one again on day 5; thereafter no amount of testosterone has any effect; the time is past. The rat is born much earlier than the human, so this period corresponds to about 12 to 14 weeks post-fertilization in man (that is, quite early in pregnancy).

Such sensitive periods in bodily development are less in evidence during postnatal growth. If adolescence has been delayed by a failure of the brain maturation mechanism or by a pituitary gland failure, then we have reason to suppose that at least a considerable degree of adolescent growth can be evoked several years later by appropriate endocrine treatment. The initiation of adolescence, in other words, is not a critical period in the sense used here. This is not to say that sensitive periods may not occur postnatally. They may do so, particularly in the growth, maturation and functioning of the brain. The subject is in need of much research, not less on the morphological and physiological than on the psychological level.

Growth gradients

One way in which the organization of growth shows itself is through the presence of growth gradients. These can be best explained by reference to

Fig. 21. Taking the simple, right-hand panel first: the percentage of the adult value at each age is plotted for foot length, calf length and thigh length in boys. At all ages covered by the data the foot is nearer its adult status than is the calf; and the calf is nearer its adult status than is the thigh. A growth gradient is said to exist in the leg, running from advanced maturity at the far end of the limb, to retarded maturity at the end nearest the trunk. The word 'gradient' has arisen because of the supposed mechanism by which such phenomena come about. It is thought that, in the embryonic limb bud, before any differences in maturity between the three segments can be discerned, there must be differences in the concentration of some chemical substance. Thus a concentration gradient of the chemical substance leads to a maturity gradient in physical structure.

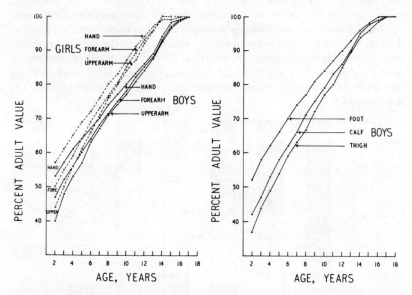

Fig. 21. Maturity gradients in upper and lower limbs. Length of segments of limbs plotted as percentage of adult value. Note hand nearer adult value than forearm, and forearm nearer than upper arm at all ages, independent of sex difference in maturity. Mixed longitudinal data from Simmons, 1944. (From Tanner, *Growth at Adolescence*, Blackwell: Oxford.)

The left-hand panel in Fig. 21 shows the same gradients in the arm, which resembles closely the leg in its whole manner of growth (one must remember that we share many of our growth patterns with other mammals, and the great majority of them with other primates, that is apes and monkeys, who have growth curves much resembling those of man); in the arm the gradient runs from hand to shoulder. Two further things may be noted: first, the sex difference in maturity appears again here, without affecting in any way the hand-shoulder gradient (for each segment of the arm girls are ahead of boys, and the same is true in the leg); second, the upper two segments of the arm are a trifle ahead of their corresponding segments in the leg; the foot, however, is as advanced as the hand, or even ahead of it.

The advancement of arm over leg reflects another growth gradient, known to everyone who has seen a newborn baby. In the newborn the head is much larger than the trunk, compared to the adult, and the legs are smaller. This is illustrated in Fig. 22, where the percentage that head-and-neck length, trunk length, and leg length contribute to total length at different ages is given. The head end of the organism, as we have repeatedly emphasized, develops first; the limbs develop last.

Fig. 22 illustrates a further point about gradients. Gradients may exist during a certain time only in development and be swamped by other processes at other times. They may also interact with other gradients, either additively, as in the sex difference gradient and the limb hand-shoulder gradient, or doubtless in some cases in a more complex fashion. In Fig. 22 the change of percentages of stature due to the three component parts is progressive until age 13; but from 13 to 17 the gradient disappears, being supplanted by a particular influence on one component, notably the adolescent spurt affecting trunk length more than head-and-neck or leg length.

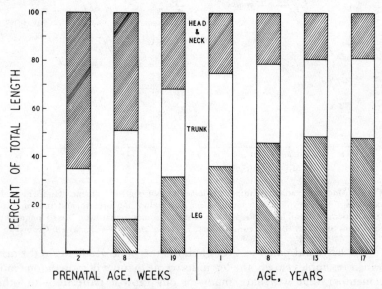

Fig. 22. Percentage of total body length due to head-and-neck, trunk, and legs in boys at various stages of prenatal and postnatal growth. Note increase in trunk percentage between 13 and 17. (Redrawn from Meredith, 1939.)

Gradients can be quite localized in their occurrence; presumably the majority are so, the ones we know about being the ones producing widely spread effects. There is, for example, a gradient controlling growth of the fingers and toes, so that the second finger is nearer maturity than the third, the third nearer than the fourth and the fourth nearer than the fifth.

There is no reason to doubt that much of the growth of the brain is organized by means of such gradients; indeed, we can identify some of them already (see Chapter 5).

Furthermore, it has been shown in animals that many adult differences in size and shape arise through the differential advancement or retardation of particular body areas, usually during fetal life. Differences between inbred strains (which are more or less equivalent to differences between individuals in human genetic terms) can often be explained in this way. Not all gradients lead to adult differences; advancement of a particular area in the fetus of one strain does not of necessity give rise to a finally greater development of that area when adult status is reached, since the more retarded strain may grow for longer or may grow faster at a subsequent time. In practice much adult variation evidently *does* depend on localized growth-velocity differences in the fetus, For example, adults of a particular inbred rabbit strain have a localized broadening of the vertebral column in the neck, relative to another strain. This difference is not only present in newborn animals, but is manifest already in fetuses 20 to 21 days after fertilization, one strain showing an earlier appearance of ossification centres in this region (Crary and Sawin, 1957).

Disorganization of growth

The multitude of chemical reactions going on during differentiation and growth demands the greatest precision in linkage. Thus for normal acuity of vision to occur the growth of the lens of the eye has to be harmonized closely with the growth in depth of the eyeball. The shape of the lens determines the degree to which the light rays are bent to a focus, and the point of focus must lie on the retina, that is the back wall of the eye. It is small wonder that the success of this co-ordination varies, and most people are just a little long-sighted or short-sighted. Again, it would seem that many features of the face and skull are individually governed by genes which do not much influence the growth of other, nearby, features. But in general the parts of the face fuse to constitute an acceptable whole, and this is because the final stages are plastic and variable, and in fitting together, for example, the upper and lower jaws forces of mutual regulation come into play which do not reflect the original genetic curves of the discrete parts (see, e.g., Kraus, Wise and Frei, 1959).

These regulative forces harmonizing the velocity of growth of one part with that of another, or the speed of one chemical reaction with that of another, do not always succeed even in arriving within an acceptable area around the target. If the original genetic forces begin by being too unbalanced, normal development cannot occur. For example, if one of the chromosomes in the human is reduplicated so that an abnormal number and distribution of genes occurs in the fertilized egg, then various abnormalities of growth occur, the best known being Down's syndrome (mongolism), a disorder comprising physical abnormalities and mental defect. An extreme example of disharmony of development is provided by the behaviour of children with pathologically precocious puberty, described in Chapter 3, where the development of the endocrine system is greatly advanced relative to that of the brain.

There are a number of child psychologists and psychiatrists, for example Bowlby (*Discussions on Child Development, Vol. IV*, p. 36; see also p.33), who think that differential variations in the speed of development of different structures and functions may explain some or many of the individual differences in personality structure, just as they explain differences in morphology. Further, some psychological abnormalities, or culturally excessive deviations from the average (analogous to an inconvenient degree of short-sightedness), are thought to arise from insufficient harmonization of the speeds with which various structures and functions develop. This could occur either for genetical reasons, the child carrying, by chance, a relatively disharmonic set of genes, or for environmental reasons, the development of one area of the personality having been speeded up by external forces, perhaps early in childhood, while another was relatively retarded.

Disharmonized development in the psychological sphere could signify simply a disharmonious development of brain structure leading to an abnormality of personality, such as the mental defect often occurring in persons with chromosomal abnormalities. Perhaps a similar, though not detrimental, disharmony of development may lead to the extreme development of a gift for music or mathematics or drawing. These gifts almost certainly depend on the intrinsic development of particular brain organizations, though to refer to these as 'structures' might be misleading, since they are probably not localized brain areas (see discussion, Chapter 5).

However, the same principle can usefully be carried further. Different psychological functions develop in an individual in a distinct order, and without begging the question of their relation to neurological structure, we can say that they too may develop disharmoniously, perhaps because of interaction between the child and his parents or teachers. Thus if the interaction necessary for the development of one psychological activity is too little, then the next activity to develop may fail to appear, or may appear late or in a distorted form. Perhaps, even, restraint applied to prevent one activity from being manifested may, by a sort of backpressure, prevent or distort the appearance of subsequent activities.

Though in our present state of knowledge it is hard to avoid lapsing, as above, from precise explanation into hydraulic analogy, this general viewpoint, nurtured in experimental embyology, clearly offers possibilities for behavioural research. Not all human behaviour is open to such a delightfully simple explanation as that of *Anser oedipoidipus* studied by Lorenz (*Discussions on Child Development, Vol. IV*, p. 128). Domesticated strains of geese mature earlier than wild geese, and in the offspring of a wild gander and a domesticated goose disharmonization occurs between sexual maturation and the earlier mother-following response. The mother-following response still remains in operation when the sexual response appears, and the young male bird in consequence insists on copulating with its mother. Since the wild father's sexual activity arises only later in the spring, it is unnecessary that he should be killed; he remains completely indifferent to the drama.

Lorenz gives a second example, also in geese, but also instructive, after the manner of an exaggerated model. Pair-formation in geese depends upon a chain of activities, beginning with those called 'distance courtship'. This is the only behaviour pattern of the chain which is different in the two sexes. Thus it sorts out heterosexual pairs, and the remainder of the courtship activity chain, culminating in mating, takes place between these pairs. Distance courtship may be omitted, for environmental reasons, or because of disynchronization, and, if so, homosexual pair formation occurs as readily as heterosexual and the pairs thus formed continue to the actual stage of mating.

Stages of development: general and singular

In child development circles there has been much argument as to whether development is continuous or whether it occurs in 'stages', that is, in jumps separated by plateaux when little happens. Again, supposing stages to exist, there is argument as to whether any *general* ones occur characterizing a simultaneous achievement of a number of anatomical, physiological and psychological developments.

Physical growth, as we have repeatedly stressed, does *not* occur in a series of jumps, but continuously (except for the minor seasonal variations seen in some children). Thus in physical growth it is clear that no 'stages', in the sense used above, exist, except in so far as one might consider the rapid change at adolescence as the achievement of a new, and mature, stage.

Nor is there good evidence for the existence of discontinuous stages of development in the brain; however, one should add here that our evidence is so scanty that stages with rest periods in between could occur without our present investigations showing them. In the development of perception in the young child no distinguishing stages have been found; here also development seems to be continuous (Piaget, *Discussions on Child Development, Vol. IV*, p. 12).

Stages are sometimes said to occur in the development of motor skills such as crawling, walking, and so forth. It is said, for example, that either a child walks or he does not walk—and this in a tone which implies that one day the child, previously unable to walk at all, suddenly finds the ability to walk unaided. Close observation of the development of such an ability, however, by no means supports this notion (McGraw, 1943, pp. 74-86); on the contrary, the ability to walk develops gradually. At first the child acquires inhibitory control over the neonatal movements of the legs, then he makes stamping leg movements when supported, then deliberate forward steps when supported, then independent steps but with the arms widely extended, feet far apart and knees flexed. Only when these developments are completed does the child walk with heel-toe progression, and still later with the arms swinging synchronously with the legs. Thus walking constitutes a 'stage' only in the sense that acquirement of the hook of the hamate, a particular feature of one of the wrist bones used in assessing skeletal age, constitutes a stage. It is an arbitrary end-point or culmination of a series of continuous developments.

The greatest application of the notion of discontinuous stages is in the field of cognitive development (Piaget, *Discussions on Child Development, Vol. IV*, pp. 11, 116). Here, if anywhere, the discontinuity may be more real than apparent. In the solution of certain problems, for example those involving the idea of conservation of matter, there seems to be little progress for a long time. A child may try to find a solution to the problem by trial and error, and may get closer to the correct solution by successive approximations. But then, rather abruptly, he changes his tactics and reasons in a logical way, giving the correct solution with a feeling that it is self-evident. A new stage has been reached, apparently by a jump in development, and the solution of a whole class of problems has become clear to the child. Even here close analysis reveals that during the apparently latent period fragments of the solution have been appearing; progress has been going on, but the integration of ability occurs suddenly.

It seems then that discontinuous stages of development occur in the human only in complex functions, that is, in functions for which many parts of the brain have to be integrated. At a simpler level the cell assemblies mature continuously, but the fusion of the constituent parts to form a whole assembly capable of handling the idea of conservation, for example, seems to take place as a jump.

In emotional development, too, stages have been described and here also the complexity of the system involved makes one feel that they may exist; but we have no certain knowledge on the point. Continuity undoubtedly underlies most of the apparent discontinuity seen in the child's development.

In some creatures, such as insects at metamorphosis, general stages of development do occur with the transitions from one to another marked by changes in morphology, physiology and behaviour. From an evolutionary point of view this is a dangerous mechanism, for the transition period is one of great vulnerability to environmental upset. In mammals, including man, no such general stages occur; even in the strictly anatomical field different systems develop in succession and with a considerable degree of independence. At birth considerable adjustments to circulation and respiration are made, yet the brain and the biochemical development of the tissues go on developing quite unruffled.

Only at adolescence in man do we have anything approaching a general stage; here, it is true, developments in anatomy, physiology and behaviour do tend to occur in a synchronized manner. But the degree of synchrony is only relative: skeletal age and dental age, it will be remembered, are linked but not absolutely, and though the processes causing advancement in the skeleton seem to be associated with those advancing mental development, they are only one small contributor to the total intellectual capacity.

Development is best envisaged as a series of many successive processes, overlapping one another in time and linked loosely or tightly as the case may be. Out of the complexity of the linkages, under equilibratory forces, emerges an overall order with visible changes in the various sectors following one another with the regularity of a continuously changing mosaic. The process is one of continuous unfolding, with speeds varying from time to time in different parts of the mosaic; it is not a succession of kaleidoscopic bumps. Only in certain restricted areas do rapid reassortments of the pieces occur, as they fall into newly integrated and increasingly precise patterns.

Prediction of adult size from size in childhood

One of the results of the regularity of growth, and of the forces restoring the child to its curve after some perturbation, is that prediction of adult height can be made from knowledge of the height in earlier years. So much is obvious enough to any parent; but the form of the curve shown in Fig. 23, and the quantitative aspects of the predictions, are interesting. The vertical scale in Fig. 23 shows the magnitude of the correlation coefficient, which is a measure of the closeness of association between two things measured, in this case height at birth, 1, 2 and so on, and height at adulthood. The coefficient covers a range from 0 (no association) to 1 (complete association; one predictable precisely from the other). The scale of the coefficient is such that it is progressively harder to raise it the higher it gets; thus the step from 0.7 to 0.8 is greater than the step from 0.3 to 0.4. The square of the coefficient gives approximately the percentage of adult variability explained by variability at birth, 1, 2, etc., or the percentage predictability. When asked to predict how tall child A was going to be as an adult, if one knew nothing about A at all except his name one would have to say that he would be between x and y inches tall, x and y being the upper and lower limits of normal adult heights. Given, however, A's 5-year-old height, which has a correlation of about 0.8 with adult height, one's prediction is narrowed to 60 per cent. of the total adult range.

Apart from its intrinsic interest to children and parents such an ability to predict may have a practical use. Children entering certain schools of ballet, for example, are required when adult to be between rather narrow height limits if they are to fulfil their hopes of joining the ballet company as dancers. They enter the school at 9 or 10, and though they receive a general education their whole orientation is toward dancing. The

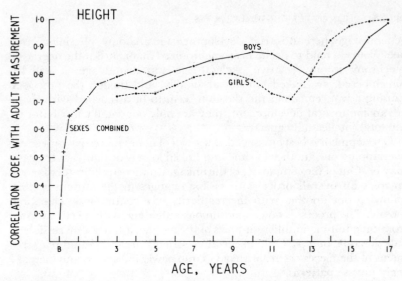

Fig. 23. Correlations between adult height and heights of same individuals as children. Sexes combined lines (0-5) from 124 individuals of Aberdeen study (Tanner, Healy, Lockhart, MacKenzie and Whitehouse, 1956) with + points from Bayley (1954). Boys' and girls' lines (3-17) from 66 boys and 70 girls of California Guidance Study (Tuttenham and Snyder, 1954). All data pure longitudinal. (From Tanner, *Growth at Adolescence*, Blackwell: Oxford.)

disappointment of those who fail to end up between the prescibed height limits, and their subsequent vocational troubles, can be easily imagined. Prediction of adult height from present height and skeletal maturity, as described below, has proved helpful in preventing the entrance of those whose chances of ending within the prescribed limits are really remote. One can place the limits as one pleases; in the situation described, those children with a 2 per cent chance, even, of ending between the limits are allowed to enter, but those with a lower chance are advised to try something else.

The form of the curve in Fig. 23 is instructive. Length at birth tells one almost nothing about adult height; but the correlation coefficient rises rapidly, and by 1 year it has reached 0.65. It continues to rise fairly swiftly till about 3 and thereafter rises only gradually. Just before adolescence begins the correlation reaches about 0.85. At adolescence predictability falls as a result of individual differences in the time of the adolescent spurt. The prediction for a boy of 5 ft. 6 in. at 13 years who has practically finished his spurt is very different from that for a boy of the same size and age who has not yet started. This difficulty can be overcome by using skeletal age instead of chronological age, a practice which is essential at adolescence. Table 1 gives the predictions based on chronological age and height only; Bayley and Pinneau (1952) and Tanner *et al.* (1975) have published further more detailed tables for prediction based upon skeletal age.

TABLE I

Mean percentage of mature height reached at each
age 3 months to 18 years. Data based on longitudinal
study of approximately 20 children of each sex,
Berkeley (Calif.) Growth Study, period 1930-1950.
(From Bayley and Pinneau, 1952.)

Chronological age		Boys	Girls
Months	3	33.9	36.0
	6	37.7	39.8
	9	40.1	42.2
Years	1	42.2	44.7
	1½	45.6	48.8
	2	48.6	52.2
	2½	51.1	54.8
	3	53.5	57.2
	4	57.7	61.8
	5	61.6	66.2
	6	65.3	70.3
	7	69.1	74.3
	8	72.4	77.6
	9	75.6	81.2
	10	78.4	84.8
	11	81.3	88.7
	12	84.0	92.6
	13	87.3	96.0
	14	91.0	98.3
	15	94.6	99.3
	16	97.1	99.6
	17	98.8	99.9
	18	99.6	100.0

At birth predictability is low because birth size depends very largely on
maternal environment and not on the genes of the fetus. During the last
month of pregnancy the fetus slows down in growth, apparently as a result
of influences from the uterus. The slowing down is related to the total
weight of the uterine contents, and twins begin to slow down earlier than
singletons. The mechanism ensures that a small mother can successfully
give birth to a child who is genetically destined to be large, perhaps from
having a large father. In the months after birth such a child grows fast,
catching up onto his true growth curve.

The rise of correlation from one year onwards seems probably to reflect
a somewhat different phenomenon and one of great importance in

principle. Not all genes are active at birth; all through life previously dormant genes awaken, or at least produce new effects that they were unable to produce at an earlier age. Some genes of medical importance show this particularly clearly. Huntington's chorea, for example, a disease of the nervous system, is due to a single gene inherited very simply and manifesting its effects with great regularity. But the disease usually appears between 30 and 40, and despite searching no clear abnormality can be demonstrated before the disease begins. It seems that a similar thing occurs in the genes governing growth. As the child grows, more of the genes show their hand; not only is the child's adult status increasingly well predicted, but his resemblance to his parents in size (relative, of course, as well as absolute) becomes increasingly marked also. Most of these height genes seem to be exerting their effects by about age 3.

Probably, however, a rather different set of genes governs the magnitude of the adolescent spurt: this would explain why the adult-child correlation rises only to 0.85 before adolescence and then increases sharply as final height is achieved. This is another example of the action of genes whose expression is age-limited, as it is called, that is, whose effects are only manifest at a certain age. Such genes—and it should be remembered that by age-limited we undoubtedly mean physiological-age-limited rather than chronological-age-limited—must certainly be of great importance in the development of the brain and the endocrine system, in underlying the emergence of certain types of ability and behaviour.

CHAPTER FIVE

Growth and Development of the Brain

We know as yet all too little about the growth of the brain and the development of its organization. Anatomical studies of brain structure are immensely laborious and few workers have had the courage, persistence and technical support needed to carry out morphological analyses of the brains of children at different ages. We owe much of our knowledge in this field to the devoted labours of Conel (1939, 1941, 1947, 1951, 1955, 1959, 1963, 1967), who has published analyses of the cerebral cortex at birth, 1 month, 3 months, 6 months, 15 months, 2 years, 4 years and 6 years. Rabinowicz (1978) has extended the series to 8 years on the one hand, and 6, 7 and 8 months of fetal life on the other. These studies were made with the optical microscope. Since Conel's time the electron microscope has enormously extended the detail with which the nervous system can be probed. A number of investigations, in particular by Drs Sidman and Rakic of Harvard University, have produced pictures of the developing nervous system whose beauty and elegance make the fashionable discipline of molecular biology look simple and lifeless. These methods are immensely laborious and suitable human material is hard to come by. Nevertheless the promise is there; gradually the immense complexity of the developing brain is being unravelled.

Physiological studies are at present practically confined to the electroencephalogram (EEG) patterns, but to date these have provided more hints as to development than solid data from proper longitudinal studies. However, the technique of recording the activity of single nerve cells has become well established, so the physiologist is now able to map very precisely the sort of cells his probes encounter.

The biochemical growth of the brain, that is the mapping of the concentrations of chemical substances at various stages of development, has advanced much in the last ten or fifteen years, but biochemical methods tend to gloss over just that detail which is the chief feature of the brain's organization. Most of the biochemical data so far concern total concentrations of substances in the whole cerebrum or cerebellum, and fail to reveal precisely where the substances are located. However, the time is certainly coming when immuno-chemical methods will allow the same sort of fine distinction between individual cells that the microscope and the tiny probes of the electrophysiologist permit.

Despite this relative lack of information, however, it is still clear, not only in principle but from particular examples, that all the mechanisms discussed in the previous chapter apply to the brain; there are growth gradients, sensitive periods, linked speeds of development, genes with age-limited expression. There is no reason to doubt that one day we shall be able to understand the development of the brain as well as the development of, say, the eye.

To what extent such understanding will illuminate the development of the mind, of mental skills and behavioural attitudes, is a matter of debate. Nobody would deny that morphology and chemical and electrical function in some way underlie mental activity. We have at present no convincing picture of the physical basis of memory, nor any precise knowledge of the changes produced in the nervous system by learning. But there seems real reason to suppose that within the next decade or two these basic problems in understanding mental function in neurological terms will be certainly much nearer solution, if not solved. Indeed, the study of the development of the brain on the one hand and the develop-ment of mental ability on the other could do much to illuminate the relations between mind and brain. Piaget and Inhelder (see *Discussion on Child Development, Vol. IV*), in particular, have described the development of psychological abilities in terms which most strongly recall those used for the maturing of structures in the nervous system; there seems little doubt that the emergence of the ability to reason by formal logic (see Inhelder and Piaget, 1958, p. 336), for example, is as much the result of the maturation of certain brain structures (not a particular area or nucleus, probably, but a widespread organized network) as is the emergence of the ability to see or touch.

Morphological development

From early fetal life onwards the brain, in terms of its gross weight, is nearer to its adult value than any other organ of the body, except the eyes. In this sense it develops earlier than the rest of the body. Its curve of growth from birth to adulthood has been given in Fig. 5 above, in comparison with the general bodily growth curve, and the curve for the reproductive organs. At birth the brain is about 25 per cent of its adult weight, at 6 months nearly 50 per cent, at 1 year 60 per cent, at $2\frac{1}{2}$ years about 75 per cent, at 5 years 90 per cent and at 10 years 95 per cent (data of White House Conference, 1933, smoothed). This contrasts with the weight of the whole body which at birth is about 5 per cent of the young adult weight, and at 10 years about 50 per cent. The velocity curve for the weight of the whole brain reaches its peak about a month before birth; deceleration is thereafter quite rapid. By 1.0 year the brain weight velocity is down to about 25 per cent of its peak value, and by 2.0 years to less than 10 per cent of its peak.

However, total brain size or weight is not a very satisfactory measurement. Different parts of the brain grow at different rates and reach their maximum speeds at different times. Fig. 24 illustrates this for the prenatal period in the same manner as Fig. 21 (p. 57), which showed the growth gradients in the upper and lower limbs postnatally. In Fig. 24 the percentages of the value at birth are plotted for the weights of the cerebrum (including the corpus callosum, basal ganglia and diencephalon, with the thalamus and hypothalamus), the cerebellum, the midbrain, the pons and medulla, and the spinal cord (for an illustration of the parts of the brain, see Fig. 27). The midbrain and the spinal cord are the most advanced at all ages from 3 fetal months to birth, and the pons

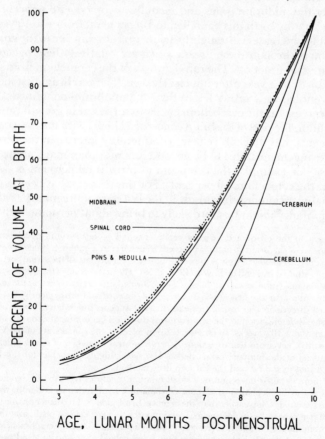

AGE, LUNAR MONTHS POSTMENSTRUAL

Fig. 24. Percentage of their volume at birth reached at earlier months by parts of the brain and spinal cord. Cerebrum includes hemispheres, corpus striatum and diencephalon. (Data from Dunn, 1921.)

and medulla come next.[1] The cerebrum is less advanced, but still much ahead of the cerebellum (Dunn, 1921: see also Noback and Moss, 1956; Dobbing and Sands, 1973; Schultz et al., 1962; Howard et al., 1969). Though data on the postnatal growth of these parts are not numerous (see Scammon and Dunn, 1924; Dobbing, 1974; Cheek, 1975), it is clear that these relationships would be essentially unchanged if the plots were made in terms of percentage of adult value; that is, no counter gradients appear, so far as is known, during the postnatal period.

Fig. 25 illustrates the same point in a different way, comparable with that of Fig. 22 above. Here the percentage of the total volume of the brain made up by cerebrum, cerebellum and midbrain–pons–medulla is plotted, from 3 months postmenstrual to 20 years after birth (data from White House Conference, 1933, Vol 1A, p.180; and see Dunn, 1921). Initially the midbrain, pons and medulla occupy over 8 per cent of the volume, but by birth this has fallen to 1.5 per cent; from 1 to 10 years the percentage increases very slightly again, presumably due to the growth of fibre tracts through these areas, which are relatively heterogeneous in structure and function. The rapid growth of the cerebellum from shortly before birth to a year after it is clearly seen. The cerebrum first increases in percentage as it grows faster than the midbrain–pons–medulla and then decreases as the cerebellum comes to surpass it in growth rate.[2] The cerebellum, the part of the brain concerned chiefly with the fine control of movements, has its peak velocity considerably later than the cerebrum (this arrangement seems to be general amongst mammals; in the rhesus monkey, for example, the cerebrum at birth is 80 per cent of its adult weight, the cerebellum 40 per cent). For this reason it has been supposed that malnutrition or other insult in the last part of pregnancy or the first part of infancy might be more likely to bring about permanent effects on

[1]Contrary to the oft-quoted 'law' of cephalocaudad or head-to-tail development, the development of the brain structures proceeds in general in a caudo-cranial (or cervicorostral) direction. A good example is the development of the nucleus of the spinal portion of the Vth nerve, studied in detail by Brown (1956, 1958). The first section of the nucleus to appear is the caudal one (subnucleus caudalis) which is formed first (at $6\frac{1}{2}$ weeks) at the caudal end of the medulla near the first cervical segment of the cord and subsequently develops in a headward direction. The rostral or head division appears much later; it also undergoes progressive differentiation in the cervicorostral direction beginning at about 14 weeks and ending at about $18\frac{1}{2}$ weeks. In fact the entire nucleus of the spinal tract of the Vth nerve develops in a cervicorostral direction. A cervicorostral sequence of development of the motor nuclei of the human cranial nerves also seems highly probable, for this has been demonstrated in the rat and the cat (see Brown, 1958).

[2] The more detailed dissection of a small number of fetuses reported by Jenkins (1921) shows that the diencephalon (thalamus, epithalamus, hypothalamus and optic tracts) and corpus striatum develop earlier than the cerebral hemispheres. The diencephalon falls from some 10 per cent of brain volume at 3 fetal months to 3 per cent at birth, and the corpus striatum similarly from about 10 per cent to about 5 per cent. Thus the cerebral hemispheres themselves increase relatively even more than is indicated by the line for 'cerebrum' in Fig. 25. The hemisphere increase of size between 2 and 3 fetal months is from about 20 per cent to nearly 70 per cent of total brain volume; at 6 fetal months the hemispheres constitute 85 per cent of total brain volume.

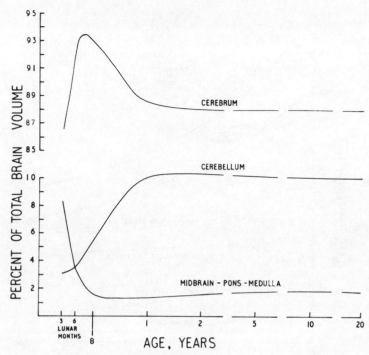

Fig. 25. Percentage of total brain volume contributed by cerebrum, cerebellum and midbrain–pons–medulla at ages from 3 lunar months postmenstrual to adulthood. Cerebrum includes hemispheres, corpus striatum and diencephalon. (Data from Dunn, 1921; White House Conference, 1933.)

movement control, making for a clumsy child, than on anything else. At present the idea is only speculative.

Finally in Fig. 26 the actual speeds of growth of linear measurements of the cerebrum (defined as above), cerebellum, and midbrain and pons during the fetal period are shown (data from Dunn, 1921, smoothed values: note that the scale for cerebellum, midbrain and pons has been doubled to give curves comparable in scale to the others). The maximum speed of growth is reached by the spinal cord, midbrain, pons and cerebral hemispheres before the graph begins, probably at a postmenstrual age of about 2 months for the spinal cord, midbrain and pons, and about 3 months or slightly before for the cerebral hemisphere dimensions. The cerebellar dimensions grow at a nearly constant rate from 4 to nearly 8 months. The shape of the curves, representing the degree of deceleration of the organs, is an additional guide to maturity; the spinal cord decelerates fast, the cerebrum, midbrain and pons less fast, and the cerebellum scarcely at all till birth.

Even these curves are still too general. The brain is made up of two

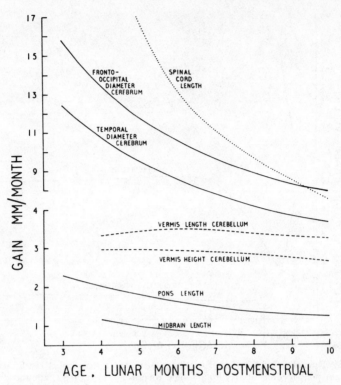

Fig. 26. Velocity curves for linear measurements of parts of brain and spinal cord from 3 months postmenstrual age to birth. (Data from Dunn, 1921, smoothed values.)

fundamentally different sorts of cells, the neurons proper or nerve cells, and the neuroglia or supporting cells. The neurons are the cells which transmit impulses. Each consists of a cell body, with a nucleus as in other cells, and a cytoplasm drawn out into a very large number of fine wire-like processes called dendrites. In most cells one such process is much larger and much longer than the others and is called the axon. In a motor nerve of the cerebral cortex, for example, the axon runs all the way down from the head to cells in the spinal cord. Axons themselves often have many smaller branches. The dendrites are mostly short and form a pattern of arborization or branching, the intricacy of which invokes comparison with stellar statistics. There are about 10^{12} or a million million neurons in the brain and the average cerebral cortex neuron would seem to have some 30,000 nerve processes terminating on it, probably coming from a tenth or so of that number of cells. The neurons are not tightly packed together like cells in most other tissues; there are narrow gaps between each, filled with tissue fluid. The connection with other cells is made through branches of an axon coming into close proximity with the dendrites of other cells, though without joining. Messages are passed across the tiny gaps by chemicals released at the nerve endings. It is thought that the most important clue to the functional capacity of a brain is the 'connectivity' of its neurons, that is the number of connections each cell makes with the others.

The neuroglia, which occupy about half the cellular volume of the brain, do not carry messages like the neurons. They are the support links, in the logistic sense, and act as intermediaries between neurons and the blood supply; a number have one process attached to a capillary blood vessel and the other intertwining among the surrounding neurons. They are smaller and more numerous than the neurons. They probably transmit glucose, amino-acids and other substances to neurons for the production of energy and the manufacture of structural protein and the chemical messengers. There is also evidence that during development some sorts of neuroglia act as scaffolding along which neurons actually move from their point of production to their final position. Other neuroglia manufacture the myelin sheaths which surround the axons. Thus neuroglia clearly have a crucial role in the nervous system.

Neurons and neuroglia develop at quite different times, at least as concerns cell division. Most of the neurons in the cerebrum are formed during the period from about 10 to 18 postmenstrual weeks; that is to say their nuclei are formed then, surrounded by minimal cytoplasm. Axon and dendrite growth comes later; in some cases, it would seem, very much later indeed. Glial cells in the cerebrum begin to be formed around 15 postmenstrual weeks and continue being formed, though at a decreasing rate, until some time in postnatal life. It is said that new neuroglia cells are formed in the cerebrum up to about 2 years postnatally, but surprisingly, in the cerebellum only up to 15 months (Dobbing, 1974). However, these are generalizations based on chemical rather than structural evidence.

Cerebral cortex development

Conel's work has provided us with an extraordinarily valuable picture of the development of the cerebral cortex from birth to 6 years and it has been supplemented by Rabinowicz's studies (1978). The cerebral cortex is identifiable at about 8 postmenstrual weeks, and by 26 weeks most of it shows the typical structure of six somewhat indeterminate layers of nerve cells (the grey matter) on the outside, with a layer of nerve fibres, the white matter, on the inside.

At first the cells are small, consisting largely of nuclei with very little cytoplasm. They are closely packed, with few and small processes. As they develop, their axons and dendrites appear; nucleoprotein material known as Nissl substance, stainable with suitable dyes, appears in their cytoplasm; and a fibrillary structure becomes visible in the cytoplasm upon silver impregnation (the neurofibrils). Many of the axons acquire an insulating sheath of myelin, the thicker fibres in general getting more, the thinner ones less, and some fibres practically none at all.

From these changes a series of criteria for maturation of parts of the cortex can be obtained, just as criteria for skeletal maturity were obtained from the changes in appearance of the ossification centres of the hand and wrist. Conel used nine criteria: (1) the width of the layers of the cortex; (2) the number of neurons per unit of volume, or density of neurons, the density decreasing as cytoplasm, fibres and inter-neuronal substance increases in area; (3) the size of the neurons; (4) the condition of the staining Nissl substance; (5) the presence of neurofibrils; (6) the size and length of axons and dendrites; (7) the presence of pedunculated bulbs, structures seen near cell bodies; (8) size and number of fibres entering the cerebral cortex from the rest of the brain and the spinal cord; and (9) the degree of myelination of the axons.

There is considerable localization of function in the cerebral cortex, certain parts being necessary for vision, others for movement, and so on. The locations of the chief areas of this sort are shown in Fig. 27. Around the primary motor, sensory, visual and auditory areas are areas known as 'association areas' which are evidently concerned with the integration of the information arriving in the primary area. Thus, if the primary visual area is destroyed blindness results; if the visual association area is destroyed things can still be seen, but the interpretation of this information is faulty, in other words the 'meaning' of the things seen is distorted, and the ability to recall visual images may be impaired. Within the primary motor and sensory areas (and perhaps the visual and auditory too) there is strict localization of different parts of the body. Thus the nerve cells which if stimulated cause the legs to move are at the top of the motor area, those for the hands lower down, and those for the face near the bottom. Similarly the last cells in the chain transmitting sensation from the legs are at the top of the sensory area, the cells for the hands in the middle of the sensory area, and so on.

Conel's studies from birth to 6 years have shown that two clear sequences or gradients of development occur during this time. The first is in the order in which these general areas of the brain develop, the second the order in which the bodily localizations advance within the areas.

The leading part of the cortex is the primary motor area located in the precentral gyrus, that is, the fold of the brain immediately in front of the chief, or central fissure (see Fig. 27). Next comes the primary sensory area in the postcentral gyrus; then the primary visual area in the occipital lobe; then the primary auditory area in the temporal lobe. All the association areas lag behind these primary motor and sensory stations. Gradually the waves of development spread out, as it were, from the primary areas; thus in the frontal lobe the parts immediately in front of the motor cortex develop next and the tip of the lobe is last in maturity. The same seems to be true of the occipital lobe and probably of the others also. The parts on the medial or inside surface of the hemisphere are in general last to develop; the hippocampal and cingulate gyri lag behind most areas of the frontal lobe, and the insula, the part of the cortex covered over by the lips

LATERAL VIEW

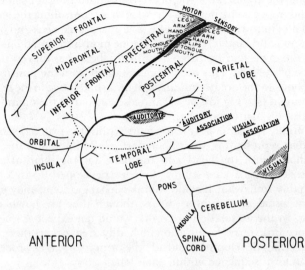

MEDIAL VIEW

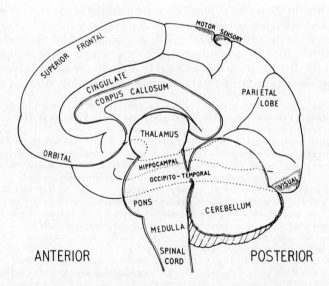

Fig. 27. Lateral and medial views of brain, to show divisions of cerebral cortex, areas of localization of function, and location of thalamus, cerebellum, pons, medulla and spinal cord. A, lateral view of cortex. B, medial view of cortex and subcortical structures. (After various maps, including Penfield and Rasmussen, 1950.)

of the temporal and frontoparietal lobes, lags behind all parts of the frontal lobe.

Within the motor area the nerve cells controlling movements of the arms and upper trunk develop ahead of those controlling the leg. At birth the order of maturity appears to be (a) upper trunk, neck and upper arm, (b) leg and hand, and (c) head; but by one month the hand has joined the rest of the arm, and by three months the head has moved up to be in advance of the legs. This order is maintained from then until 2 years; it corresponds to the greater maturity of the arm relative to the leg in bodily development (see Fig. 21, p. 57) and also, of course, the infant's capacity to control his arms more than his legs.

Essentially the same gradient occurs within the primary sensory area. The areas representing the upper part of the body and the arms lead throughout, with the head and the hand joining them at around six months. The leg area remains the least developed up to 2 years and presumably somewhat beyond. Similar local gradients may exist in the primary visual and auditory areas, though they are nowhere near so striking. In the association areas one would not expect gradients of this sort, since little or no localization by bodily areas occurs there. Conel, in fact, describes development outside the primary areas as proceeding in a fairly uniform sequence within each lobe.

The actual status of the cortex from birth to 2 years may be summed up as follows. At birth no Nissl substance and few neurofibrillae are to be seen anywhere in the cortex (though they are plentiful in the cells of the spinal cord and in the brain below the cortical level). A small amount of myelin is present in the primary motor, sensory, visual and auditory areas; but the appearance in general does not suggest that cortical function is possible.[1] By one month considerable maturation has occurred in the motor cortex, particularly in the upper limb and trunk area, but

---

[1] The sequence of myelination in the human spinal cord and brain has been studied by Langworthy (1933) and others (e.g., Keene and Hewer, 1931; Yakovlev and Lecours, 1967). Myelin first appears at about 14 postmenstrual weeks in the motor cranial and spinal roots, the medial longitudinal bundle and the first sensory pathways. The sensory pathways from the lower limbs (fasc. gracilis) myelinate later than those from the arms and upper trunk (fasc. cuneatus), corresponding to the relative state of bone and muscle development of the two areas. By the time viability of the fetus is reached at the seventh month (i.e. the time when it can survive outside the uterus) most cranial nerves and most nerve tracts descending down the cord are myelinated, together with the vestibular system, the roof nuclei of the cerebellum and the ascending spino-cerebellar tracts. But there is no myelin above the midbrain level and none in the cerebellar cortex or dentate nucleus fibres. The cervical region of the spinal cord is more mature than the lumbar region. At the eighth month the fibres in the corpus striatum, rubrospinal tract and vermis of the cerebellum become myelinated, and a small amount of myelin appears in the thalamus. There is still little present above the level of the IIIrd nerve nuclei and none in connections to the cerebral cortex. At birth the optic nerves, and the pathways to the cortex, have a small amount of myelin, and the thalamus has more than previously. By two months myelination of the optic tracts is complete, and the olfactory tracts, geniculate bodies and pyramidal tracts have begun to myelinate. The ventral, but not yet the anterior or medial nuclei of the thalamus have some myelinated fibres. By five months, according to Langworthy, all the tracts have

elsewhere the appearances still suggest limited, if any, function. By three months all the primary areas are relatively mature, suggesting that simple vision and hearing are functional at a cortical level but not at a level involving any interpretive functions dependent upon the association areas. By six months most areas have advanced further and many of the exogenous fibres coming to the cortex have become myelinated; but the majority of the association fibres passing from one part of the cortex to another are still immature. The hippocampal gyrus has begun to mature, but the cingulate gyrus and the gyri of the insula appear still unlikely to be able to function.

Between six and fifteen months the rate of development is greatest in the temporal lobe and the cingulate and insula; next greatest in the occipital, and least in the parietal and frontal lobes, which have already passed through most of their course. Though the primary motor area is still in advance of all others the differences between it and the rest are now becoming reduced. Considerable maturation has occurred in the association areas, particularly the visual one, which is still ahead of the auditory. The macula area (that is the area corresponding to the exact centre of fixation and point of clearest daylight vision in the retina) is the most advanced of all the visual areas. The area in the frontal lobe concerned with eye movement is now well developed, but other portions of the frontal lobe remote from the primary motor area are still relatively immature.

By 2 years the primary sensory area has caught up with the motor area. The association areas have developed further, but the visual is still ahead of the auditory, suggesting that there is more discriminative ability in vision than in hearing. In the frontal lobe the mid-frontal gyrus immediately opposite the hand motor area is more advanced than the superior frontal, which in turn is more advanced than the inferior frontal and the orbital cortex. The trunk, upper limb and head areas in both motor and sensory regions are still clearly ahead of the leg areas; evidently the leg areas do not catch up till 3 years at the earliest. The hippocampal and cingulate gyri are developed to about the same degree as the superior frontal lobe, but the insula is still less mature than any part of the frontal, and brings up the rear amongst these divisions of the cortex.

It is clear from the studies on myelination by Yakovlev and his colleagues that the brain goes on developing in the same sequential fashion at least till adolescence and perhaps into adult life. Myelination of nerve fibres is only one sign of maturity, and fibres can and perhaps sometimes do conduct impulses before they are myelinated. But the information from myelin studies agrees with Conel's information on

some sign of myelination, though in a great number, of course, the process is far from complete. It should be remembered here that myelination of a fibre is not absolutely essential to its function and fibres can conduct impulses before they have acquired their myelin sheaths; however, it is clear that in general the beginning of myelinization and the beginning of function do take place at approximately the same time.

nerve cell appearances where the two overlap. As a rule the fibres carrying impulses to specific cortical areas myelinate at the same time as those carrying impulses away from these areas to the periphery: thus maturation occurs in arcs or functional units rather than in geographical areas.

A number of tracts have not completed their myelination even three or four years after birth. The fibres which link the cerebellum to the cerebral cortex and which are necessary to the fine control of voluntary movement only begin to myelinate after birth, and do not have their full complement of myelin till about age 4. The reticular formation, a part of the brain especially developed in primates and man and concerned with the maintenance of attention and consciousness, continues to myelinate at least until puberty and perhaps beyond. Myelination is similarly prolonged in parts of the forebrain near the midline. Yakovlev suggests that this is related to the protracted development of behavioural patterns concerned with metabolic and hormonal activities during reproductive life.

Throughout brain growth from early fetal life the appearance of function is closely related to maturation in structure. Fibres of the sound-receiving system ('the acoustic analyser') begin to myelinate as early as the sixth fetal month, but they complete the process very gradually, continuing until the fourth year. In contrast, the fibres of the light-receiving system, or optic analyser, begin to myelinate only just before birth but then complete the process very rapidly. Yakovlev points out that in fetal life the sounds of the functioning of maternal viscera are the chief sensory stimuli, apart from anti-gravity sensation. They are evidently not perceived at a cortical level; but at a sub-cortical one the analyser is working. After birth, however, visual stimuli rapidly come to predominate, for man is primarily a visual animal. These signals are very soon admitted to the cortex; the cortical end of the optic analyser myelinates in the first few months after birth. The cortical end of the acoustic analyser, on the other hand, myelinates slowly, in a tempo probably linked with the development of language. Rabinowicz's data on the density of cells in the second and fifth layers of the cortex agree with this interpretation. Throughout all parts of the brain studied, cell layer 5 is ahead of cell layer 2 on this criterion, and in the primary visual cortex layer 5 progresses faster between six postmenstrual months and birth than any other brain area. By three months after birth the appearance of this layer of cells is adult; the same layer in the auditory area reaches adult appearance some three to six months later.

In short, there is plenty of evidence that in the brain functions appear when structures mature, and not before. There is no reason to suppose that the truth of this generalization suddenly ceases at age 2, or 3, or 13. On the contrary, there seems every reason to suppose that the higher intellectual abilities of the brain also appear only when maturation of certain structures is complete. These structures must be units of organization widespread through areas of the cerebral cortex, rather than local areas like the motor area. Their maturation is probably signified both by increasing size and myelination of some cells and fibres remote from the primary centres and by an increase in connectivity. The latter must predominate more and more as the child gets older, since the actual increase in volume of the brain gets less and less. But dendrites, even millions of them, occupy little space, and very considerable increases in connectivity could occur within the limits of a total weight increase of a few per cent.

The stages of mental functioning described by Piaget and Inhelder and the emergence of mental abilities (to avoid using their word 'structure' to denote the substratum beneath the ability) have all the characteristics of developing brain or bodily structures (see Piaget, *Discussions on Child Development, Vol. IV*, pp.11-116). The stages follow in a sequence, which may be advanced or delayed as a whole but not altered, just as in the case of a wrist bone or a cortical primary area. Stage 2 includes the characteristics of Stage 1, which is equally like wrist or cortex. The higher stage involves also 'integration' of previous stages with the emergence of possibilities of function at a more complex and developed level; this also applies to cortical maturation and to the development of neuromuscular mechanisms. There seems every reason to suppose that Piaget's successive stages depend on progressive maturation or at least organization of the cortex. Environmental stimulation may or may not be necessary to create the required cell assemblies (see on). For the cognitive stages to emerge brain maturation is probably necessary, but not, of course, sufficient. Without at least some degree of social stimulus the latent abilities may never be exercised. As Inhelder and Piaget (1958, p.336) themselves put it: 'The appearance of formal thought (at adolescence) . . . is a manifestation of cerebral transformation due to the maturation of the nervous system . . . (But) the maturation of the nervous system can do no more than determine the totality of possibilities and impossibilities at a given stage. A particular social environment remains indispensable for the realization of these possibilities. It follows that their realization can be accelerated or retarded as a function of cultural and educational conditions.'

In the emotional development of the child no such clear-cut scheme of development stages exists, though several attempts to delineate something more or less similar have been made (e.g., Erikson, *Discussions on Child Development, Vol. III*, p. 169). Here again maturation of the cortex must assuredly play a large role in permitting the passage from one type of behaviour to another. The psychosexual behaviour of the 6-year-old boy with precocious puberty and fully adult secretion of sex hormones, described on p. 40, provides one example of this. But our knowledge in this field is practically non-existent and we must await the results of future research.

Hemispheric specialization

The two hemispheres of the human brain are not simply mirror images of each other. Some tasks are predominantly done by one side, some predominantly by the other. In processing of language (both in the sense of reception and of production) the left hemisphere is the dominant one, apparently from an early age. In processing of spatial information, either visual or tactile, the right hemisphere plays the major part. Recently Witelson (1976) has found evidence of a sex difference in the genesis of this second laterality. Boys from at least age 6 (the lowest age tested) process tactile spatial information better in the right hemisphere; girls process equally well in both sides at least till 13 (the highest age tested). The average of the two sides was the same for both sexes. This work needs confirmation and extension, but may be of considerable importance in demonstrating a pre-pubertal sex difference in brain function, in the sense of one sex specializing earlier than the other. Boys have long been known to have a higher incidence than girls of reading and language defects, and the former at least involves spatial as well as linguistic processing. It would be quite in keeping with other aspects of sex differences if the male specialized away from the basic pattern, and ran some excess risk in doing so.

Influences on brain development

Granted that new brain functions, perhaps including the higher intellectual ones, coincide in appearance with the development of brain structure and organization, which comes first, which causes the other? A short and elementary answer would be a clear one: maturation occurs first and psychological function follows.

Many examples could be given of how maturation of the nervous system occurs quite independently of any exercise or learning. In lower animals embryos have been raised under continuous narcosis which prevented them from making any of the spontaneous movements that usually occur. Even though the overt expression of a whole series of precursor steps of behaviour had thus been suppressed, normal behaviour patterns appeared as usual; the behavioural steps were clearly only manifestations of underlying intrinsic developments and not in any way practice steps (see Weiss, 1950, p.28). Lorenz (*Discussions on Child Development, Vol. I*, p. 52) has described a similar maturation of flying movements in birds. Young pigeons were kept in cages which prevented the occurrence of incipient flying movements (which is a not too abnormal situation, since these birds are naturally cave-breeders). Pigeons of the same brood reared without this restriction begin to fly at a certain time, but at first fly only to a perch a short way up, then the next day higher, the day after higher still and so on, till after some days the full ceiling, represented by circling in the air, is achieved. One might think the pigeons were practising or learning flying movements. But this is not so; for the restrained birds, if released on the final day, soar straight up and circle as do the others, their flying ability complete.

In man also the process of maturation is unaffected, so far as we are aware, by exercise of the centres concerned. Premature babies, for example (excluding those born prematurely by reason of some defect), become able to stand and to walk no sooner for being longer exposed to the stimuli of the outside environment. Calculated from birth, they reach these milestones later than babies born at term, but calculated more correctly from fertilization, they reach them at just the same time (Douglas, 1956). Micturition in man has much in common with the flying response in pigeons, from a maturational and experimental point of view. In identical twins early training of one child to the pot produced no earlier achievement of dryness than occurred in the co-twin subjected to little or no training (McGraw, 1943, p. 123).

This is not to say by any means that maturation of the brain is unaffected by any outside conditions. The outside conditions involved, however, seem likely to be general ones, such as malnutrition or the presence of toxic substances. Conel remarks that at all ages some infants' brains were more myelinated than others, and this was general over the whole cortex and not particular to one area. Evidently individuals vary in the rate at which they lay down myelin, just as they vary in the rate at which they lay down calcium in the bones of the wrist. Conel also remarks that several of the infants with the least myelin for their age had a malnourished appearance. To what extent malnutrition can retard brain maturation in man is the subject of much current debate, some of it heated (see Chapter 6). In rats both malnutrition and lack of thyroid hormone cause delayed maturation of the brain and delayed neuromuscular functioning (Eayrs and Horn, 1955; Eayrs and Lishman, 1955). Lack of thyroid hormone certainly does in man, as evidenced by cretins. It would be interesting to know if the brains of girls were more mature than those of boys at birth and indeed throughout growth, as are their skeletal systems. But data on this are lacking. At birth they are more advanced in activities leading to creeping, sitting and walking, though by five months boys have drawn level (Campbell and Weech, 1941). On average, girls acquire control of their bladders earlier than boys, and their later motor development is said also to be generally in advance, as instanced by such things as the ability to tie bows or to skip.

If learning and exercise are without effect, then, on at least the more simple aspects of brain growth and development, have they any effect at all on brain structure? Are the effects of learning represented only by physiological adjustments—reverberating nerve circuits, domain patterns, and so forth? Can learning during the growing period of the brain influence the brain's development in structure? Perhaps not; but with the qualification that earlier ages *may* be more plastic than later ones, and that the distinction between the sort of structural change we are now discussing and reverberating circuits and domain patterns may be a meaningless one. The problem is similar to that of the neural basis of memory, which equally admits no positive answer at present.

J.Z. Young (in Weiss, 1950, p. 103) and others have suggested that the size of a nerve cell is partly determined by the amount of stimulation falling on its dendritic field. The motor cells serving muscles with few sensory endings leading back to their dendrites are smaller than cells serving muscles with many sensory endings, such as the anti-gravity muscles. But the existence of the sensory endings, and not the amount of their stimulation may in fact be the deciding factor. The functional significance of large as opposed to small cells is in any case unknown.

Cajal, the great pioneer of cortical histology, believed simply that learning was associated with the growth of axons and dendrites, activity being assumed to stimulate that growth. On this basis he accounted for the retention of childhood memories and the loss of recent memories in the aged, the pathways formed during childhood being supposedly the most durable (see Sholl, 1956, p. 82). A more modern exponent of an essentially similar view is Hebb (1949) who proposes that repeated firing of a cell B by cell A induces some kind of growth of the axon terminations of A such that the further passage of impulses from A to B is facilitated. The theory accounts for persistence of memories, and it is certainly true that very slight changes in the dimensions of the processes of a neuron could lead to great differences in its pattern of connectivity. But there is no positive evidence that use, during childhood or at any other time, does in fact cause dendrites or axons to grow.

The reader by now may be reflecting ruefully on the lack of positive information available from the biologists. However, in the last few years a body of knowledge has emerged which indicates, perhaps, the beginning of a real understanding of how the nervous system generates its fantastically intricate and precise patterns.

Much of the evidence has come from studies of the visual system. In all mammals very precise connections are made from the retina to the occipital part of the cerebral cortex, with a cross-over wiring system ensuring that both eyes are represented at each point of the cortex. Thus objects in space, which form images in both eyes, generate impulses from each eye which end up exciting precisely the same nerve cells in the cortex. The visual cortex, indeed, consists of millions of columns or slabs of cells arranged with crystalline regularity, each column being a cellular machine equipped to analyse the visual events that occur in a tiny portion of each retina. The location in space of the event is given by the identity of the particular slab activated and the neurons in the slab analyse what type of event is occurring. The problem is to discover how this quite extraordinary regularity has been generated during growth.

An equal regularity is seen in a portion of the brain called the geniculate body, which is simply a relay station for nerves on their way from retina to cortex. The first set of fibres terminate there and the impulses are taken up by a second set of neurons which pass them on to the visual cortex. Now, in the rhesus monkey, the cells of the geniculate body are all generated within the space of a few days during fetal life, and Rakic has shown that at first they are not separated into their distinct layers. The fibres from the left and right retinae arrive, and to begin with all is confusion, fibres from one side being diffusely intermingled with fibres from the other. Gradually the ordered chess-board pattern emerges, with clusters of fibres from one side alternating with clusters from the other. Experiments in other species have led to the belief that two sets of endings terminating on one neuron must somehow exchange information as to their precise place of origin. On this information depends the retention or loss of the endings. It is not too difficult to imagine how this might happen in an animal subjected to visual experience during this time; if two terminations were often activated simultaneously (because they represented corresponding parts of the retinae) they would persist; if not, one would die or at least become inactivated. It is more difficult to understand how this could occur in the darkened world of the embryo. Hubel and Wiesel at Harvard have shown that in the monkey the whole elaborate structure of the visual system is complete before birth. However, covering one eye in the visual cortex from birth onwards results in a diminution of the number of cell terminations subserving the covered side and an enlargement of the clusters of terminations from the other side. If the eye is covered for a year no recovery is possible. It seems that nerve cells, like muscles, atrophy from disuse.

In the cat, much of the architecture is complete before the eyes are opened, but Blakemore and others at Cambridge University have demonstrated that the cell connections required for precise binocularity or stereopsis of vision need the stimulus of visual experience. They have also shown that a kitten brought up in a world consisting exclusively of vertical stripes develops many more cortical cells which analyse this dimension of shape than cells which analyse the horizontal dimension (whereas normally both are present equally).

Furthermore, it seems that during development some axons form transient connections with a whole series of cells before establishing their stable adult contacts. In toads, for example, the eye moves its position relative to the head during growth, and in order to register an image seen by the two eyes onto the same area of the brain as the eye grows, a series of cell contacts are successively made and broken. In addition there is evidence in adult mammals that axons entering the spinal cord from the periphery make a much wider series of connections in the spinal cord than are illustrated in the anatomical textbooks. These terminations seem normally to be suppressed; they remain, in Merrill and Walls' phrase, as 'ghosts of the cells' childhood'. The conditions under which they may be activated again are not clear.

Mark, of the Australian National University, whose book *Memory and Nerve Cell Connections* is a masterly exposition of the field, sums up the new view thus: 'The principle of supplying, by growth, an overabundance of nerve cells or synaptic connections and fixing the final patterns by discarding many of them seems to show up often in the development of the nervous system, especially in the fine details of connection formation.' Dendrites seem no longer such static processes; perhaps even in the adult they may be built and broken.

Whatever the truth or falsity of Hebb's notion that use actually alters the structure of cell processes, there is no doubt that in the brain associations of nerve cells, diffuse in location but linked in function, are built up progressively during the course of growth. These cell assemblies are thought of as having relative stability in the sense of maintaining their many constituent cells. Perceptual learning, for example learning to distinguish a square from a triangle irrespective of size or colour, is achieved gradually during growth. At birth the cortex is virtually non-functional and it may be imagined that in the months that follow cell assemblies are built up under the joint influence of the internally unfolding maturation, providing now one cell ready for function, now another, and of the stimulus of the environment. The maturation factor would be largely or wholly inherited, and would determine the size of the assemblies for evaluating music, for example, or recognizing perspective. The development of the ability to abstract perceptive constancies—that is, to recognize a bird as a bird from all angles and at all distances—has much in common with the development of reasoning, as Lorenz and Piaget have said *(Discussions on Child Development, Vol. IV,* p.106). Neurophysiologically speaking, these abilities may develop in the same way.

The question remains unanswered as to whether optimal size or permanence of an assembly is secured by giving particular stimulation to it at a particular time, or whether assemblies built early in childhood are under most circumstances more resistant to decay or change than later-built ones, as one might suppose on behavioural grounds.

Physiological development of the brain: the electroencephalogram during growth

The only important data on the physiological development of the brain in children come from the electroencephalogram (EEG). The EEG records the electrical currents produced in the brain under a variety of circumstances. The currents recorded by electrodes fixed to the scalp necessarily represent a mixture of the currents produced by the various parts of the cortex and diencephalon, and a mixture attenuated and distorted by passage through the membranes, bones and skin. Nevertheless it is possible to record currents from different parts of the scalp and to follow at least to some extent the spread of waves of excitation through the brain. Tumours, for example, can often be accurately located if they produce abnormal waves.

Again, the waves produced are of a very varied nature, and simple inspection of an EEG record, even by an expert, gives less information than some form of statistical analysis by mechanical means. The usual analyser counts the number of waves per second which fall into different frequencies; in other words, carries out a Fourier analysis. It is not known whether in fact the complex record is produced by a summation of waves of these different frequencies; it need not be, since the analysis is by no means unique. However, it provides a method for classifying the records accurately, if nothing else.

At birth the waves recorded are large in amplitude and low in frequency, mostly below 7 cycles/second. This is called delta activity. As the child gets older, spends longer periods awake and pays more attention to his surroundings these slow rhythms become more intermittent, being increasingly replaced by waves smaller in amplitude and faster in frequency, the alpha rhythm. By age 5 the alpha rhythm predominates most of the time. Higher frequency waves appear more and more, shifting the average rate gradually upwards from about 8 cycles/second at age 6 until the adult average of about $9\frac{1}{2}$ cycles/second is reached some time around 11 to 13. Girls differ slightly from boys in their frequency spectrum, a distinction which may arise towards adolescence, although this is not certain (see Tanner, 1962).

The alpha rhythm has been characterized as accompanying a 'search for pattern' (Grey Walter in *Discussions on Child Development, Vol. I*, p. 140) and its development obviously does relate to the maturing of the brain and the development of perceptual and cognitive capacities. But more than this one can scarcely say at present. Well-controlled longitudinal EEG studies on children, using modern methods of recording and stimulation by lights and other devices to test the dynamic response rather than the resting state, are conspicuous by their absence.

The accepted picture of physiological development of the brain (see e.g. Hebb, 1949, p. 124) is one wherein at first unstimulated neurons, probably grouped in chains or pools, fire spontaneously as metabolic states build up to and pass a threshold. The big slow waves of the delta rhythm probably reflect this. But as the cells become stimulated their spontaneous discharge becomes a rarer and rarer occurrence; they are brought under afferent, that is to say environmental, control. Inititally this control is exerted over the sensory areas; but it is extended gradually into the association areas until they, too, come under environmental control. This is regarded by Hebb as the stage of primary learning. The larger size of association areas relative to primary sensory areas in the human brain may explain the slowness of initial learning in man as compared with, say, the rat, and may be one of the most important developments permitted by the great prolongation of childhood in the human.

Individual differences in brain maturation and the IQ

Large individual differences occur in the rates of maturation of the skeleton, in the growth to maturity in height, and in every other aspect of growth about which we know anything. It would be quite astonishing if they did not equally occur in the development of the brain, and we have every reason to suppose that they do. The differences in overall myelina-

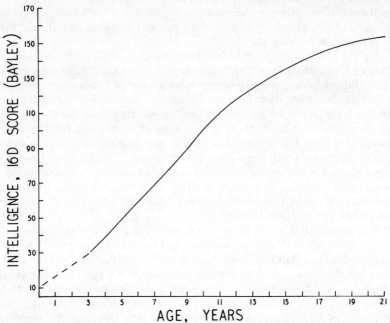

Fig. 28. Growth curve of intelligence test score suggested by Nancy Bayley (1956) on basis of children followed from birth to age 21 in Berkeley Growth Study. Means and standard deviations at all ages adjusted to mean and standard deviation of this group on Wechsler-Bellvue test at age 16 (hence '16 D score'). Redrawn from Bayley, 1956.)

tion of the cortex from birth to age 2 described by Conel have been remarked above. Evidently some children myelinate more rapidly than others; probably some grow their dendrites faster; probably some grow their cells and connections faster in particular areas; and so on.

Individual differences in those aspects of behaviour that we can measure seem to be smaller at birth but have considerably developed, through differential speeds of growth, by the age of two months (McGraw, 1943, p. 115). Thus the various stages leading to creeping, sitting and walking are passed at different times by different children just as the stages of bladder control, speech and the eruption of teeth.

The same differences of tempo of growth—partly determined by heredity and partly by the degree and kind of environmental exposure—undoubtedly exist in passing the stages of cognitive and reasoning ability described by Inhelder and Piaget (1958) and the more conglomerate measure of abilities represented by the Binet intelligence test. Any growth curve of test intelligence must have something arbitrary about it, since the items of the test are not the same at all ages, and indeed prior to age 3 or 4 are fairly radically different from what they are later. Nancy Bayley's (1956) standardization of the test results from a longitudinally followed

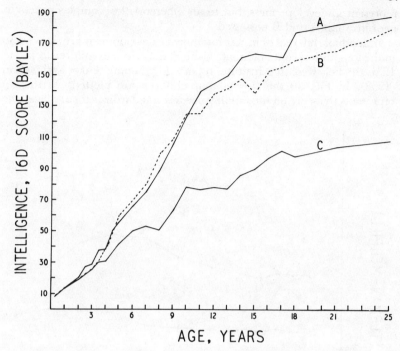

Fig. 29. Growth curves of intelligence test score (Stanford-Binet and Terman-McNemar adjusted to means and standard deviations of Wechsler-Bellvue at age 16) of three children followed longitudinally from birth to age 25. (Redrawn from Bayley, 1956.)

sample of the Berkeley Growth Study children, given in Fig. 28, is probably the most satisfactory curve constructed to date. Its shape should be compared with the distance curves for various organs and tissues of the body given in Fig 5 (p. 22). At once it will be seen that the test intelligence curve resembles most the curve of brain growth. It rises at first less steeply—as on Hebb's hypothesis of primary learning it perhaps should—but otherwise its shape closely follows the shape of the brain curve.

In discussing measures of maturity in Chapter 3 a deficiency inherent in present-day intelligence tests was mentioned (see p. 36). These tests fail to differentiate between advancement and actual ability. The distinction may be seen by reference to the three curves reproduced in Fig. 29 from Bayley's longitudinal data. Here individual A scores some ten to fifteen points higher than B from age 9 onwards; but from 4 to 9 he scores less. Furthermore, the shape of the curves would have inclined one even at 18 to predict that the 9 to 18 difference arose largely from A's advancement, and that the final scores might well be a good deal closer than the 18-year-old ones. Such turns out to be the case, at 25. Individual C, on the other hand, had a lower IQ at all ages than A and B; his 'backwardness' was not due to retardation, unless we quite unrealistically assume all low IQs to represent undevelopedness, but to an inherently less complex system of neurons than A and B possessed.

Individual differences in test intelligence development are shown also in the longitudinal data of Stanford-Binet tests given to children from 3 to 12 at the Fels Research Insitute, reported by Sontag, Baker and Nelson (1958). In Fig. 30 the IQs of four children are plotted. As the IQ represents the score on the intelligence test standardized for age level, the

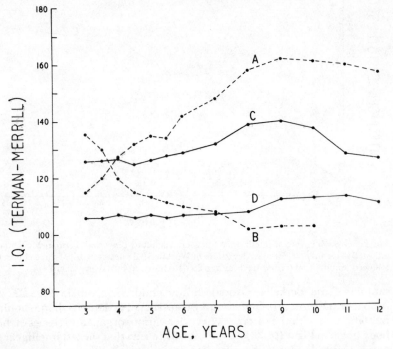

Fig. 30. Growth curves of IQ (Terman-Merrill) of four children followed longitudinally from age 3 to 12. Children A and B represent approximately the maximum gain and loss in IQ in the 140 children studied. Data from Sontag, Baker and Nelson (1958).

child who is repeatedly just average at every age obtains a constant IQ and his data plot is a straight line. If all children developed at the same rate all the 140 children's lines given in Sontag and his colleagues' monograph would be straight lines parallel to the horizontal axis, some high, some medium, some low.[1] But in fact some children consistently

[1] This is an over-simplification: owing to the occurrence of different standard deviations at each age, slight variation above and below the line would in fact occur. But it would be concomitant variation for all the children. Some IQs are now reported as 'deviation IQs', that is IQs adjusted for the different standard deviations at each age. In deviation IQs children developing at the same rate would have IQs describing straight parallel lines. Deviation IQs are reached, essentially, by finding the centile status of the child at the age given and converting this back into an IQ by making the 50th centile IQ 100 and the 2.5th and 97.5th IQs 70 and 130 respectively.

increase their IQ over all or most of this age range (A); some consistently decrease (B); some increase and then fall back again (C); and most stay fairly constant (D). (The reader should be warned that A and B represent practically the extreme gain and fall in this group of 140; changes of this magnitude are unusual.) Some of these changes in IQ are due, no doubt, to environmental changes, parental pressures, and such like. Some of the trends are probably due to some children having a greater need for competitive striving to master their environment than others; this is the explanation of the long-term trends most favoured by the authors. But (even though each point represents a smoothed 3-point moving average) the trends shown in the curves seem too regular all to be explained in this way. Part of the cause must certainly be differences in rate of development of mental ability, correlated with differences in rate of development of the brain itself.

CHAPTER SIX

Interaction of Hereditary and Environmental Factors in Controlling Growth

Growth is a product of the continuous and complex interaction of heredity and environment. Modern biology has no use for simplistic notions, and statements such as 'height is an inherited characteristic' or 'intelligence is the product of social forces' (or vice versa) are crudely misleading. What is inherited is the DNA of the genes. Everything else is *developed*.

In modern genetics it is a truism that any particular gene depends for its expression firstly on the internal environment as created by all the other genes, and secondly on the external environment. Furthermore, the interaction of genes and environment may not be additive; that is to say, bettering the nutrition by a fixed amount may not produce a 10 per cent increase in height in all persons irrespective of their genetical constitution, but instead a 12 per cent rise in the genetically tall and an 8 per cent rise in the genetically short. This type of interaction, wherein a particular environment proves highly suitable for a child with certain genes, and highly unsuitable for a child with others, is called non-additive. (A critical period of development, requiring an external stimulus, as described in Chapter 5, may be regarded as an extreme example of non-additive interaction, an environment devoid of the necessary stimulus being intensely unfavourable to the genotype that requires the stimulus.) It is exceedingly difficult to specify quantitatively the relative importance, therefore, of heredity and environment. In general the nearer optimal the environment, the more the genes have a chance to show their potential actions, but this is a general statement only and undoubtedly many more subtle and specific interactions occur, especially in growth and differentiation.

The facts of interaction lead to a principle, from which the reader may deduce, if he wishes, a whole social philosophy. Everyone has a different genotype. Therefore, for optimal development (optimal, that is, for the individual, and his environment considered individualistically) everyone should have a different environment. This is of course impossible; but one may seek either to optimize the interaction or to minimize it. In relation to cattle and other domestic animals we minimize the variation in both genotype and environment, aiming at a uniform product of maximal usefulness to ourselves. Such a strategy is quite foreign to successful evolution, and is fraught with the greatest danger. Should ecological circumstances change, there will be no reserve of genotypes more suited to the new circumstances, no way forward and no way back. The true patrimony of a species is its genotypic variation.

So much for general principles. It is DNA, not stature, nor blue eyes nor even blood group A that is inherited. The sequence in the cell goes

DNA→RNA→Amino Acid assembly→protein.

The protein escapes from the cell to influence other cells in building a tissue or organ; the organ interacts with others in the embryo and fetus; the fetus interacts with the uterine environment; the child interacts with the complex and changing environment of the adult-created and self-created world. If we talk, simply, about cellular proteins, the steps from genotype to character are small and well protected. In everyday language one may certainly say that the blood group A protein is inherited. But beyond this the going is not so simple. It is a long way from the possession of certain genes to the development of a height of two metres, say. For such a character the only valid statement is thus: 'X per cent of the variation in the height of young adults brought up in the circumstances of comfortably-off urban homes in the temperate climate of central Holland in the 1960s is due to genotypic variation'. For similar young adults brought up in Saharan African villages X would be less, for the environment would intervene more decisively.

Genetical factors, however, are clearly of immense importance in the control of growth and they will be discussed first (see Tanner, 1960). The effects of race and climate and season of the year will then be given, and lastly the effects of nutrition, illness, exercise, and psychological disturbance.

Genetics of size, shape and tempo of growth

Factors affecting the rate of tempo of growth must be considered separately from factors affecting the size, shape and body composition of the child. The genetical control of tempo seems to be independent of the genetical control of final adult size, and, to a large extent, of final shape. Equally, environmentally produced changes in tempo do not necessarily affect final size or shape. Indeed, size and shape themselves seem to be separately controlled, both by genetical and by environmental factors. The gentical control of shape is much more rigorous than that of size, presumably because shape represents chiefly the number of cells in particular places, while size represents more the size of the various cells. The number of cells is fixed early, in the relative security of the uterus; the size of the cells continues to alter during much of childhood and in some instances, such as the fat cell, throughout life.

Monozygotic twins, who have the same genotype, usually resemble each other very closely indeed when brought up under similar circumstances. Table 2 shows the average differences in length or height from birth to 4 years between pairs of monozygotic and of dizygotic same-sexed twins, from the magnificent data of Wilson (1976). Dizygotic same-sexed twins resemble each other genetically no more closely than brothers or sisters, since they arise each from a different fertilized ovum. At birth the monozygotic pairs were actually less alike than the dizygotic, but this situation rapidly changed. The increasingly close similarity of the values in monozygotic twins reflects size, shape and tempo combined. The difference between pairs at birth is probably partly due to asymmetical division of the original ovum, one twin getting just a little more cytoplasm than the other, and partly to their different positions in an overcrowded uterus. The twin who is smaller at birth, by however little, usually remains smaller throughout life. On average monozygotic twins are slightly smaller than singleton children.

The degree to which height is controlled by genotype when environmental circumstances are adequate is reflected in the variation within families compared with the variation amongst a population. The range of variation in adult height, represented by ±2 standard deviations around the mean, is about 25 cm for most male populations, 16 cm amongst brothers and 1.6 cm amongst monozygotic twins brought up together. Height is generally said to be controlled by many genes, each of small effect. This is because the distribution of height in the population is continuous and Gaussian. However, as few as five or six genes suffice to produce such a distribution, so the matter is open.

Little is known about the genetics of shape. Some body measurements show higher correlations between parents and grown-up children than others. In a recent study of 125 Belgian families containing 282 grown-up children, Susanne (1975) found the correlations partly displayed in Table 3. In height each parent contributes equally to each offspring; despite all popular belief to the contrary, there is no tendency for daughters to resemble more their mothers and sons their fathers: the four correlation coefficients (0.52, 0.47, 0.52, 0.53) do not differ significantly. Other data fully bear out this generalization. Further down the table, the correlations for bi-iliac diameter (hip width) closely resemble those for height. But the biacromial diameter (shoulder width) values are less similar. The father/son correlation is very low, and the father/daughter is lower than mother/daughter. Amongst the head measurements, head breadth resembles height in pattern though all the correlations are a bit lower. But in head length the father's correlation seems especially low, and in nose length brothers resemble each other not at all.

Interpretation of these correlations is not entirely straightforward. Measurements much affected by environment have low correlations; relatives simply do not resemble each other very much. If a measurement is chiefly controlled by a few genes of which one or more shows dominance

TABLE 2

Mean differences between lengths of monozygotic twin pairs (n 140 pairs) and same-sexed dizygotic twin pairs (n 90 pairs) from birth to 4 years, and within-pair correlation coefficients. (From Wilson, 1976.)

| | Mean Difference in length (cm) | | Correlation in length | |
	MZ pairs	DZ pairs	MZ pairs	DZ pairs
Birth	1.8	1.6	0.58	0.82
3 months	1.4	1.6	0.75	0.72
6 months	1.3	1.9	0.78	0.65
1 year	1.3	1.8	0.85	0.69
2 years	1.1	2.4	0.89	0.58
3 years	1.1	2.9	0.92	0.55
4 years	1.1	3.2	0.94	0.60

(that is a single dose gives the same effect as a double dose) the correlations decrease. The presence of sex-linked genes (that is genes on the X chromosome) causes the sister-sister correlation to exceed the brother–brother correlation; the father-daughter to exceed the father-son; and the mother–son to exceed the mother–daughter. No example of this appears in the table. What is clear is that different measurements show different degrees and patterns of familial resemblance. These differences cannot be understood until the development of each measurement is studied and the physiological factors controlling its growth are clarified.

Not all genes are active at birth. Some are not switched on till later, and the products of others can express themselves only in the physiological surroundings provided by the later years of growth. Some genes only produce their effect in one sex, usually because the gene product needs the co-operation of either one or the other hormonal environment in order to exert its action. These genes are called 'sex-limited'. The effect may not be all-or-none: the type of central baldness that is quite common in men depends on a gene which in single dose causes an effect in males only. In double dose, which rarely occurs, it produces a similar effect in women.

Sex-limited genes are quite distinct from genes that are sex-linked. The sex-linked genes produce an effect that is not limited to one sex but affects alternately males and females in successive generations (so-called 'criss-cross inheritance').

Genes whose expression is age-limited may well be responsible for the fact, pointed out in Chapter 4, that children grow to resemble their parents more as they grow older, relatively as well as absolutely. In fact, the curve for the correlation of parents' height with the height of their children at increasing ages is very similar to that of a child's height with his own height when adult, shown in Fig. 23 (p. 64). The correlation is

TABLE 3

Correlations between measurements of parents and grown-up children: 125 Belgian families. (From Susanne, 1975.)

Measurement	Parent–Child	Brother–Brother	Sister–Sister	Father–Son	Mother–Daughter	Father–Daughter	Mother–Son
Height	0.51	0.53	0.57	0.54	0.47	0.52	0.53
Arm Length	0.49	0.37	0.51	0.47	0.57	0.53	0.39
Sitting Height	0.37	0.21	0.35	0.41	0.39	0.29	0.38
Biacromial Diameter	0.33	0.42	0.46	0.09	0.50	0.33	0.41
Bi-iliac Diameter	0.49	0.49	0.45	0.51	0.53	0.43	0.49
Head Breadth	0.35	0.37	0.32	0.42	0.33	0.41	0.22
Head Length	0.28	0.36	0.44	0.18	0.40	0.34	0.37
Nose Length	0.31	0.00	0.44	0.32	0.26	0.34	0.35
Interpupillary Breadth	0.38	0.34	0.40	0.32	0.40	0.42	0.38
Ear Height	0.31	0.26	0.43	0.24	0.33	0.32	0.39

very low at birth and rises sharply to about 3 years, by which time evidently much of the genes' contribution to the child's growth is manifest. A similar curve has been reported for the parent–child correlations of intelligence tests (Honzik, 1957), and it may have the same explanation.

Tempo of growth

The genetical control of tempo is manifested most simply in the inheritance of age at menarche.[1] Identical twin sisters, with the same genes, reach menarche an average of 2 months apart. Non-identical twin sisters, with the same proportion of different genes as ordinary sisters, reach menarche an average of about 12 months apart. The sister–sister and mother–daughter correlation coefficients are both about 0.4, which is only slightly below the same correlations for height. These are indications that a high proportion of the variability of age at menarche in populations living under West European conditions is due to genetical causes. Further, the inheritance of age at menarche is probably transmitted as

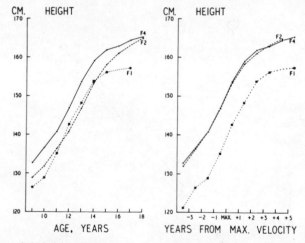

Fig. 31. Growth in height of three sisters. Left, height plotted against chronological age; right, against years before or years after maximum velocity. Note the coincidence of curves of F2 and F4 when equated for developmental age, right. Data from Ford (1958). (From Tanner, *Human Growth*, Pergamon Press.)

[1] For many studies on growth rate, age at menarche is used. This is partly because it is a definite landmark in the great majority of girls and partly because valid means and standard deviations can be obtained for different groups by the cross-sectional method of simply asking all the girls between the ages of 9 and 17, whether or not they have yet menstruated. This avoids the difficulty of depending on memory. Because age at menarche is distributed in a population in a Gaussian or near-Gaussian curve (except for a very few excessively retarded individuals probably pathological) a probit or logit transformation can be made on data of the have/have-not menstruated variety and the means and standard deviations thus estimated.

much by the father as by the mother, and is due not to a single gene but to many genes each of small effect. This is the same pattern of inheritance as that shown by height and other body measurements.

This genetical control evidently operates throughout the whole process of growth and the conclusions regarding age at menarche apply equally to rate of development in general. Skeletal age, for example, shows a very close resemblance in identical twins at all ages. In fact, under reasonable environmental circumstances, the genetical control extends down to many of the details of the velocity and acceleration curves. This is demonstrated by the records of three sisters given in Fig. 31. The heights are plotted on the left against chronological age and on the right against developmental age as represented by years before and after maximum velocity of adolescent growth. Two of the sisters have curves which are almost perfectly superimposable one on the other except that they are on a different time base, one being almost a year in advance. These two

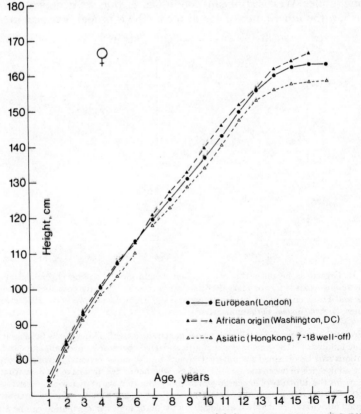

Fig. 32A. Heights of European girls, girls of African origin living in Washington, DC (USA), and well-off Chinese girls in Hong Kong.

sisters differ radically therefore in one parameter of their growth curve, but little in the other parameters. This is additional evidence also that genes controlling *rate* of growth are wholly or partly independent of those controlling final size achieved.

The time of eruption of the teeth, both deciduous and permanent, is genetically controlled, and there is evidence that the order in which teeth calcify and erupt is influenced by heredity also. This implies the existence of symmetrical factors acting locally on one or a few teeth only, an example of local growth gradients discussed above, which in the majority of cases are evidently genetically determined.

We have already seen that not all genes are active at birth. Some express themselves only in the physiological surroundings provided in the later years of growth. It is very probable that the magnitude as well as the timing of the adolescent spurt is genetically controlled, perhaps by genes causing secretion of large or small amounts of androgenic hormones. Such

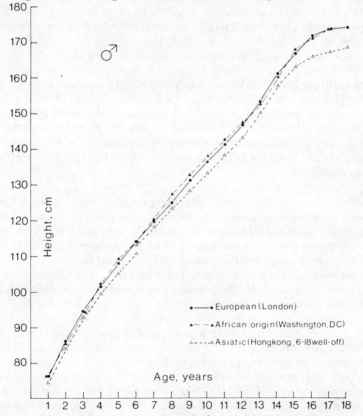

Fig. 32B. Heights of European boys, boys of African origin living in Washington, DC (USA), and well-off Chinese boys in Hong Kong.

genes may have excited no effect before the moment when the pituitary gland signals the beginning of androgen secretion.

Differences between races

Fig. 32 shows the height curves of London children, well-off Chinese children in Hong Kong and Afro-Americans from Washington, DC, who, though from a relatively low-income group in the United States, enjoyed a more favourable environment than any African group studied in large numbers in Africa (the Nigerian well-off group approach this condition however, see page 106). The European and Afro-American groups have almost identical curves for boys; the African-descended girls, however, are a little larger than the European girls. This is partly due to their having a swifter tempo, with menarche about 0.3 years earlier.

The Asiatic boys and girls are distinctly less tall, despite coming from high socio-economic groups receiving better-than-average care. It is not growth delay that makes them smaller; indeed, their tempo of growth is significantly faster than that of Londoners, with menarche at 12.5 compared with 13.0 years. Hence the adult height difference is greater than the childhood difference, not less. The difference is due mainly to differences in gene pool. A frequently quoted finding, due to Professor William Greulich of Stanford University, is that Japanese children growing up in Los Angeles were taller than Japanese growing up in Japan. This was indeed the case in the 1950s but by now the marked trend towards increasing height in Japan has eliminated the difference. Japanese in Japan, Hawaii and California no longer differ significantly in height; but both differ from Hawaians or Californians of European or African descent, their mean heights being at about the 15th centile of the British standards.

Bodily proportions. The largest differences between races, when all are growing up in good environments, are those of shape. Fig. 33 shows lines representing sitting height means at successive ages plotted against leg length means at the same ages, in boys. The London boys (solid line) show a straight line up to adolescence, at which time sitting height spurts more than leg length, causing the line to bend upwards. The Chinese when small have a similar body proportion, but by adolescence their sitting height has become considerably greater for a given leg length. The Africans, on the other hand, have a much lower sitting height for leg length (or, equivalently, longer legs for similar sitting height) and the Australian Aboriginals have still longer legs than the Africans. These characteristic differences are shown by females as well as males.

An equally characteristic difference between European and African is in the relation of shoulder width to hip width. The African has slimmer hips for a given shoulder width in both sexes. The proportions of the Asiatic in this respect are similar to those of Europeans. There are differences in body composition also, Africans having more muscle and

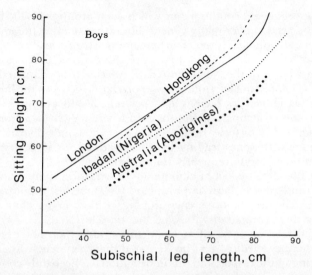

Fig. 33. Relation of sitting height to leg length in boys of different population groups. Note long legs of Nigerians, and still longer legs of Australian Aborigines.

heavier bones per unit weight, at least in males. These differences confer distinct advantages and disadvantages in certain sports, with results that can be seen in Olympic records. Africans have an advantage in many track events, especially the high hurdles, and the Asiatics an advantage in gymnastics and weight-lifting.

Tempo of growth. The African newborn is ahead of the European in skeletal maturity and motor development. He maintains this advance only for some 2 or 3 years in most areas of Africa, but this is simply because nutritional disadvantage supervenes. In America and Europe the African stays in advance in bone age and also in dental maturity. In a nationwide survey of the United States, in which a true proportionate sampling of the whole population was attempted, the median ages of menarche were 12.5 years for African-descended, and 12.8 years for European-descended. Well-off Asiatic groups have as fast a tempo as Africans, in later childhood if not in the early years. Mean age of menarche in well-off Hong Kong girls was found by Francis Chang and his associates to be 12.5 years. In Japan in the nineteen-sixties a large sample of girls from several urban areas gave a mean value of 12.9 years.

Climatic and seasonal effects on growth

It could be argued that the differences in growth that exist between Europeans, Africans and Asiatics might be due to the direct effects of climate on the growing child, were it not that we are able to compare descendants of Africans and Europeans living in the same area. The differences in growth have indeed been brought about in response to the different ecological conditions in which each group evolved, but they arose by selection over many generations rather than by the immediate effect on individual children. The long limbs of the African enable him to lose more heat per unit volume than the European, and the thick-set body and short limbs of the Northern Asiatic are similarly adaptive in arctic regions. There is, in fact, quite a close correlation between the linearity of peoples, as judged by their weight per unit height as adults, and the average annual temperature of the area where they live, or from which they migrated in historical times. Thus over thousands of years children and adults with genes leading to climate-adaptive characteristics survived to breed more frequently than others.

Only one direct effect of climate on growth is certainly known. The high altitude of the Peruvian altiplano (4000 metres) induces a larger than normal chest circumference and bigger lungs in Quechua children growing there compared with Quechua on the sea coast.

One alleged climatic effect has achieved a certain notoriety; nineteenth-century medical text-books stated that menarche was earlier in girls living in the tropics and this information has been duly copied from one textbook to another till quite recently. In fact, modern statistics make it clear that climate has little if any effect on age at menarche: people living in tropical countries mostly have in fact a late menarche, but simple because their nutritional level is low. Well-off children in temperate zones, and children of temperate-zone parentage growing up in the tropics have menarche at a normal time for the population from which they are drawn. A list of median ages of menarche in different populations is given in Table 4.

Season of the year, however, exerts a considerable influence on velocity of growth, at least in West European children. Growth in height is on average fastest in spring and growth in weight fastest in autumn. This applies at all ages after the first year. Prepubertal children grow on average three times as fast in their fastest three months (usually March to May) as in their slowest three months (usually September to October) (Marshall, 1971).

The months of greatest increase in weight in the Northern Hemisphere are usually September to October and in these months the weight increment may be four or five times the weight increment in March to May. A small percentage of children actually lose weight in the spring months. There is, however, some rather inconclusive evidence that well-nourished children show a smaller seasonal difference in weight gain than the less well-nourished.

The trends described are the average curves obtained from children followed longitudinally. Relatively few individual children have curves which coincide with these; the time of year at which different individuals have their seasonal peak varies considerably and so does the degree to which seasonal peaking occurs at all. In some individuals' records regular seasonal fluctuations occur, as illustrated in Fig. 34 for a pair of identical

TABLE 4

Median ages of menarche (years) in various population groups. (All data refer to period between 1960
and 1975: status quo method, with medians calculated by probits or logits.) Sources of data will be
found in Eveleth and Tanner (1976) and Oduntan *et
al.* (1976).

Europe		*Near East and India*	
Oslo	13.2	Bagdad (well-off)	13.6
Stockholm	13.1	Istanbul (well-off)	12.3
Helsinki	13.2	Tel Aviv	13.2
Copenhagen	13.2	Iran (urban)	13.3
Netherlands	13.4	Tunis (well-off)	13.4
NE England	13.4	Madras (urban)	12.8
London	13.0	Madras (rural)	14.2
Belgium	13.0		
Paris	13.2	*Asiatics*	
Zurich	13.1	Burma	13.2
Moscow	13.0	Singapore (average)	12.7
Warsaw	13.0	Hong Kong (well-off)	12.5
Budapest	12.8	Japan (urban)	12.9
Romania (urban)	13.3	Mexico	12.8
Carrara, Italy	12.6	Yucatan (well-off)	12.5
Naples (rural)	12.5	Eskimo	13.8
European-descended		*Africans*	
Montreal	13.1	Uganda (well-off)	13.4
USA, all areas	12.8	Nigeria (Ibadan; university-	
Sydney	13.0	educated parents)	13.3
New Zealand	13.0	South Africa (urban)	14.9
Pacific		*African-descended*	
New Zealand (Maori)	12.7	USA, all areas	12.5
New Guinea (Bundi)	18.0	Cuba, all areas	13.0
New Guinea (Megiar)	15.5	Martinique	14.1

twins whose height velocity was consistently greater in the February-
August periods than in the August-February ones. But in other children
little sign of any seasonal effect is seen. Probably the effect is chiefly due to
variations in hormone secretion, with individual differences caused by
differences in endocrine reactivity. Light, or some radiation falling on the
eye, is involved, for Marshall and Swan (1971) have shown that totally
blind children failed to synchronize their growth-rate variations with the
time of year, though the variations themselves occurred to the same
degree as in sighted children.

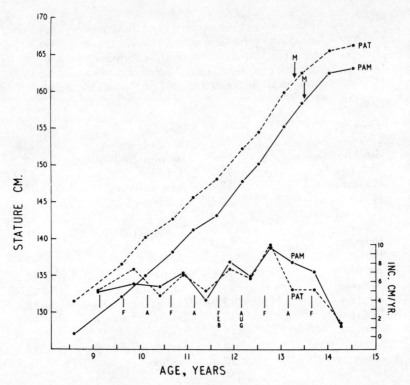

Fig. 34. Growth in height of identical twin girls, showing seasonal effect on rate of growth. From Tanner, *Growth at Adolescence,* Blackwell: Oxford.

In tropical countries seasonal variations tend more to be governed by the rainy and dry periods and follow food supply and the frequency of infections.

Nutrition

Malnutrition during childhood delays growth, as has repeatedly been shown by the effects of famine associated with war. In Fig. 35 the heights and weights of school children in Stuttgart, Germany, are plotted at each year of age, for the years 1911 to 1953. There is a uniform increase at all ages in both measurements from 1920 to 1940 (see the next chapter on this), but in the later years of the Second World War this trend is sharply reversed as the food intake of the children became restricted. After 1947 conditions greatly improved and this is reflected in the increased size of the children who by 1953 had at most ages reached or exceeded the 1939 levels.

Children have great recuperative powers, provided the adverse conditions are not carried too far or continued too long. During a short period of malnutrition the organism slows up its growth and waits for better

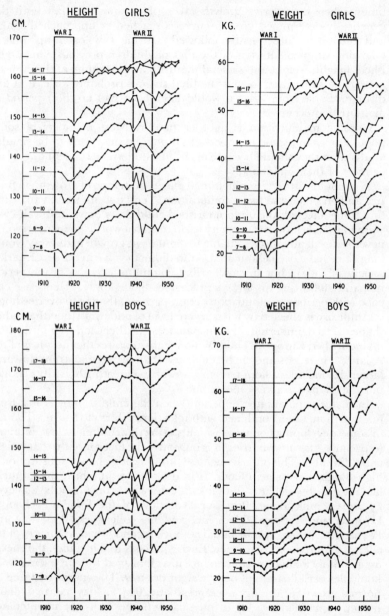

Fig. 35. Effect of malnutrition on growth in height and weight. Heights and weights of Stuttgart schoolchildren (7-8 to 14-15 Volkschule; 15-16 upwards, Oberschule) from 1911 to 1953. Lines connect points for children of same age, and express secular trend and effect of war conditions. (Data from Howe and Schiller, 1952, and personal communication.) (From Tanner, *Growth at Adolescence*, Blackwell: Oxford.)

times; when they arrive growth takes place unusually fast until the genetically-determined growth curve is reached or approached again, and then it is subsequently followed. During this 'catch-up' phase, following supplementation of the diet of children previously malnourished, height, weight and skeletal maturity are caught up at the same or nearly the same rate, so that the final stage is probably little, if at all, distinguishable from what it would have been had no short period of malnutrition occurred.

Chronic malnutrition is another matter. Most members of some populations, and some members of all populations, grow to be smaller adults than they should because of chronic undernourishment during all or most of their childhood.

We should distinguish nutritional effects on tempo of growth, on final size and on shape and tissue composition. Tempo seems usually to be the first thing affected; the undernourished child slows down and waits. All young animals have the capacity to do this; in a world where nutrition is never assured, any species unable to regulate its growth in this way would long since have been eliminated. Man did not evolve in the supermarket society of today, but in small tribal communities, most of the period nomadic, following an always precarious food supply. (Hence we can cope with periodic malnutrition better, perhaps, than with overfeeding.)

Adult size is affected by a less severe level of undernutrition than adult shape. Indeed, undernutrition in man does not alter shape significantly; a malnourished European child by no means acquires the short legs of the Asiatic. There is some slight evidence that the secular trend towards larger size includes a faint tendency towards increasing linearity of build, but the change is a very minor one.

In many populations the period when the child is most at risk from malnutrition, often combined with infection, is birth to 5 years. Though in some developing countries weights at birth are already low, in many (especially African countries) it is only after the first 6 months that weight gains diminish. This often coincides with weaning and the substitution of high-starch, low-protein foods. It is also the age at which the mother's lactating ability declines so that satisfactory growth cannot be achieved by breast milk alone. Professor Waterlow of the London School of Hygiene and Tropical Medicine, and his colleagues (Waterlow and Payne, 1975) there and in Jamaica, have recently made estimates of the energy requirements of infancy. Energy is measured in joules; the energy usage simply for bodily maintenance in a child aged 1.0 year averages 330 kilojoules per kilogram of body weight per day. The energy required for normal growth at this age averages about 20 kj/kg/day. Normal infants use up some 80kj/kg/day in physical activity. Thus the maintenance requirement is a surprisingly high percentage of the whole. When calorie intake falls below 330 kj/kg/day, as it quite commonly does in children in developing countries, then growth ceases. Even before this the energy margin for physical activity is eroded, and in the infant and child the restriction on exploration play and social interaction that follows may be a more potent cause of delay in intellectual and emotional development than any nutritional effect on the nervous system.

Protein intake seems less critical than was once thought. A child aged 1.0 year needs about 1.3 grams of milk protein per kilogram body weight; of this seven-eighths is used for maintenance and one-eighth for growth. If intake falls below this, growth ceases in 1 to 2 days. In the first six months, when the growth rate is higher, about three-eighths is used for growth. The protein/energy ratio in breast milk is about 7.5 per cent in the first few weeks, falling to 5 per cent at 2 to 3 months. This seems to be about the ratio required for healthy growth in childhood, and it is supplied by the majority of foods, including cereals.

Fig. 36 shows Dr Margaret Jane's (1975) work on the growth in height of two groups of boys in Ibadan, Nigeria. One group was drawn from the professional, highly educated classes, living in considerable style; the second from indigent slum-dwellers in the market area of the town. The curves have been drawn on British standard charts. The well-off grow very similarly to British boys while the 50th centile for the poor is no higher than the 10th centile of the British. There is no evidence that the two groups differ much in genotype though they certainly differ in other things besides nutrition. However, the major cause of the great difference in growth curves is certainly nutritional level.

The question whether undernutrition during fetal life or during the first 1 or 2 years after birth necessarily leads to an adult deficit in size or in mental function has been frequently and sometimes heatedly discussed. It seems that children with severe protein-calorie malnutrition in early infancy due to malformations or malfunction of the gut (pyloric stenosis, cystic fibrosis) make a complete recovery in height after surgical correction when brought up in reasonably well-off homes in a developed country. In the majority of studies, they had also caught up completely in intellectual ability, when assessed at ages 7 to 10 years.

Evidently much depends on the circumstances after the severe episode of malnutrition is over. Children under 5 years old admitted to hospital in tropical countries with severe malnutrition (kwashiorkor or marasmus) have been followed up after leaving hospital. In most such children complete equality of height and weight with sibling controls has been attained before puberty. In trying to isolate the effects of malnutrition from general social effects, siblings are more satisfactory controls than the general population, since they suffer some at least of the same environmental circumstances. Naturally, the children admitted to hospital come from poorly-off families where even the siblings are growing relatively badly.

Dr Steven Richardson of the Albert Einstein College of Medicine, New York, sums up the present situation very precisely in two generalizations.

Where the histories of both the severely malnourished child and the comparison child suggest a similar level of nutrition over their life histories except for the presence or absence

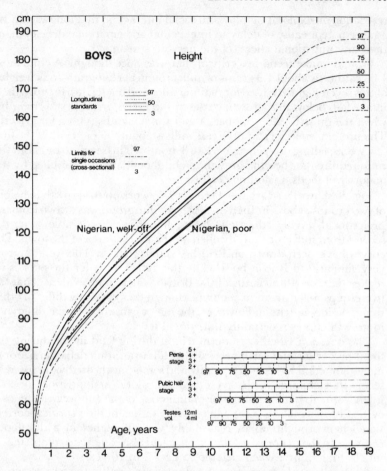

Fig. 36. Comparison of growth of well-off and urban slum-dwelling Nigerians in Ibadan. The 50th centiles of the well-off and the poor groups are plotted on British Standards. (Data from Dr M. D. Janes.)

of an acute episode requiring treatment in hospital, and where both sets of children have experienced similar social, physical and biological environments, the children with an acute episode of malnutrition will not be smaller in somatic growth than their comparisons . . . Where the children with an early acute episode of malnutrition are more disadvantaged than their environments, then the malnourished children at school age will be smaller in somatic growth than their comparisons.

He adds, however, that his own work suggests that the second generalization needs qualification: 'Even when the children with acute malnutrition come from environments and backgrounds that are somewhat disadvantaged, complete catch-up may still occur' (Richardson, 1975).

A very well-controlled study of the long-term effects of undernutrition during fetal life was made by Stein and Susser and their colleagues (Stein *et al.*, 1975) of Columbia University, New York. Between mid-October 1944 and May 1945 the central part of Holland, including the towns of Rotterdam, Amsterdam and Leiden, was subjected to a severe war-time famine. The official daily ration was 1500 calories and the actual amount eaten only slightly more than this. Examination of the birth records in these three towns by monthly cohorts of birth showed that birth weights diminished by 9 per cent in the cohorts who were exposed to the undernutrition in the third trimester of pregnancy (that is from 6 to 9 months). Those exposed only in the first or second trimesters showed no birth-weight reduction. Birth length was reduced by 2.5 per cent and head circumference by 2.7 per cent in the third trimester cohort. Maternal weight was 10 per cent less than the control values of after May 1945.

At age 19 the males of this group of children were inducted into military service. At induction their height was measured and several tests of mental ability were administered. In addition the incidence of mild and severe mental retardation was ascertained for the relevant cohorts. Susser and Stein found that young men who had been undernourished in fetal life were no different in height, weight or mental ability than those who had not been undernourished. Nor was the incidence of mild or severe mental retardation any greater. They searched for differential effects of the famine exposure according to social class, family size and birth order, and found none. Their final conclusion is an impeccable summary of the present position: 'We believe we must accept that poor *prenatal* nutrition cannot be considered a factor in the social distribution of mental competence among surviving adults in industrial societies. This is not to exclude it as a possible factor in combination with poor *postnatal* nutrition, especially in pre-industrial societies' (*Famine and Human Development*, p. 236, their italics).

Experimental models. A considerable amount of experimental work on animals has been done, designed to throw light on this question. As a result many and sometimes strident claims to certain knowledge have been made, especially in relation to effects on the highly important and emotive subject of brain growth. Such claims should be treated with the utmost caution; our real knowledge in this area at the present time is not at all great.

An early difficulty was the naivety of physiologists about species differences. Much of the early experimental work was done on the rat, a species whose growth is about as different from man's as it is possible to find amongst the whole range of mammals. Rats are born at a far earlier stage in development than primates, at an age roughly corresponding to 16 postmenstrual weeks in man. Thus, immediately postnatal undernutrition in the rat corresponds, if to anything in man, to undernutrition of the fetus in mid-pregnancy. This does not result from maternal undernutrition (unless at catastrophic levels) but only from pathology of the placenta, a wholly different situation. Besides this, the rat bears litters, not singleton fetuses, its whole endocrine system develops in a very different way from that of man, and there are enormous differences in behaviour and brain function.

Monkeys are much more suitable models, and in the last ten years they have been used increasingly in nutritional experiments. All primates have the same characteristic growth curve, although monkeys are born at a more developmentally advanced stage than apes, and apes at a more developmentally advanced stage than man. Endocrine development in monkeys is not dissimilar from man's and even the brain shares many of man's preoccupations.

In one series of experiments on Cebus monkeys at Harvard University newborn monkeys were separated from their mothers at birth and reared in a primate nursery with other monkeys. For the first 8 weeks they were fed a commercial human baby food and thereafter a synthetic liquid formula of which the control monkeys had as much as they wished. Undernutrition began at this time in two experimental groups, one simply fed 67 per cent of the controls' diet and the other fed a very low-protein diet (2.8 per cent of calories as protein) but in as large a quantity as desired. The three groups were followed for 20 weeks, then the two experimental groups were rehabilitated, eating as much of the control diet as they wanted. By the end of the 20-week experimental period the controls had doubled their weight, the calorie-deficient had increased their weight by 20 per cent and the protein-deficient had scarcely gained weight at all.

Extensive physical measurements were made on these monkeys so that changes of shape as well as size could be followed. The growth of all parts of the skeleton slowed down, and did so to a greater extent in the protein-deficient than in the calorie-restricted group. Some growth occurred in nearly all skeletal measurements, however, even in the worse-off group. Those skeletal dimensions which were farthest along their road to maturity were held up most. 'In response to malnutrition', write the authors, 'the available resources are expended disproportionately in favour of parts with the greatest distance to cover in the future ... in longterm malnutrition such a distribution would tend to lead to a closer approximation of "normal" adult skeletal proportions than would a more uniform reduction of growth rates' (Fleagle et al., 1975). The second point is an important one: the arrangement is adaptive, in the biological sense of preserving the competitiveness of the species in the struggle for reproductive success. If we assume that the normal shape of Cebus adapts it optimally to its ecological niche then the response to chronic undernutrition, a circumstance clearly encountered very frequently, should be such that the advantages of normal morphology are preserved as closely as possible. What is sacrificed is size, what is preserved is shape. The same is seen in human malnutrition.

The results of rehabilitation have not yet been reported in full. Catch-up growth is rapid in both groups, however, and by 22 weeks of rehabilitation (1 year of age) limb catch-up was complete in the calorie-deficient group and nearly so in the protein-deficient. Though we must await the final report, it seems likely that size and shape in the end returned to normal.

These experiments had another and highly instructive side. In real life undernutrition of human infants almost invariably occurs in combination with social deprivation in conditions of poverty. Hence, when such infants are treated in hospital and returned to their families and re-tested months or years later it is extremely difficult to know whether any deficit in intellectual or emotional functioning is really due to the malnutrition itself or to the effect of the associated social circumstances. Even comparison with siblings who did not enter the hospital raises the obvious problem of whether one child is favoured over another.

The Harvard investigators tackled this problem by dividing the experimental groups of Cebus infants on restricted diets each into two sub-groups. One sub-group was reared in partial isolation, that is in a solitary cage within sight and sound of other monkeys; the other sub-group was housed similarly but had three hours of play every weekday with other monkeys in a large play-pen, plus daily human handling. The monkey analogues of intelligence and emotional poise in humans are perhaps not easy to define; exploratory behaviour was the item chiefly studied, plus motor behaviour, general activity and the occurrence of items such as rocking, clutching of the body and frowning, which signify emotional disturbance. By the end of the 20-week period of food restriction it was clear that well-fed and socially deprived animals scored about the same as ill-fed and socially enriched ones, both sub-groups scoring lower in all items than the well-fed, socially enriched. 'These findings', write the authors, 'are consistent with many others in showing that the behavioural consequences of malnutrition are similar to those of emotional deprivation. The effect of suffering both conditions is more severe than either alone but in an additive rather than an interactive relationship' (Elias and Samonds, 1976). The retardation of behavioural development was less than that of growth in body size, though probably little less than that of skeletal maturity.

From a practical point of view the outcome of the monkey experiments and of those human experiences which are carefully controlled seem to agree in suggesting that events *subsequent* to a period of malnutrition occurring either in late fetal or early postnatal life exert an overridingly important effect on its outcome. The restorative powers are very great, provided social circumstances allow them full play.

Bigger not better. One last important point needs to be made here. It should not be uncritically assumed that bigger means better. Just because in temperate, industrialized countries the better-off members of the community are larger than the worse-off and tall women have more successful reproductive histories than short women, it does not follow that the same holds true under other ecological conditions. In the harsh environment of the Peruvian Andes, it is the small mothers who have more surviving offspring. Small body size may be more adaptive under some types of conditions. In an agricultural peasant economy a small man is more efficient than a tall one, requiring to do less work to feed himself. Level of nutrition has to be seen as part of the whole ecology, a whole philosophy even. Overnutrition is no less lethal than undernutrition, and a great deal more prevalent in many parts of the world. Recent evidence suggests that overfeeding in the first year or 18 months may be a contributory cause of adult obesity. In industrialized countries and increasingly in others too, bottle feeding has taken place of breast feeding and this carries with it the risk of excess, both in volume and in concentration of foodstuff.

Illness

Minor and relatively short illnesses such as measles, influenza and even antibiotic-treated middle ear infection or pneumonia cause no discernible retardation of growth rate in the great majority of well-nourished children. In children with a less adequate diet they may cause some disturbance, though this has not been securely established. Often the children with continuous colds, ear disease, sore throats and skin infections are on average smaller than the others, but inquiry reveals that they come from economically depressed and socially disorganized homes where proper meals are unknown and cleanliness too much trouble. The small size is more likely to be due to malnutrition than to the effects of the continued minor diseases (Miller, Court, Walton and Knox, 1960).

Major illnesses which take the child to hospital for a month or more or keep him in bed at home for several months may cause a considerable slowing down of growth. The mechanism by which they do so varies from one disorder to another; in a number changes in endocrine balance are probably involved and in particular an increase in cortisol secretion from the adrenal glands which if sufficient is known to slow down growth. When recovery takes place a 'catch-up' period occurs. A chronic disease may result in a considerable reduction in body size, just as does chronic malnutrition; but body proportions seem to be largely unaffected, as shown by comparison of identical twins one with and the other without the chronic disease in question.

Exercise

Though some writers have claimed that exercise increases the rate of growth or permanently enlarges the muscles, the published evidence is not sufficiently critical to allow of any firm conclusion. In adults muscles enlarged by heavy weight-lifting exercise soon regress to the pre-existing level when the exercise is stopped (Tanner, 1952) and there is little to suggest that muscular exercise in children would cause a lasting muscular enlargement. Much more research, and in particular more critical and adequately designed research, is needed in this field before any conclusions can really be drawn. A recent multi-author book edited by Rarick (1973) provides a useful perspective, even if the authors have varying degrees of acuity.

Psychological disturbance and growth rate

That adverse psychological conditions may cause a degree of retardation in growth is a thought that readily comes to mind. Clear-cut experiments on this are very hard to find, however, and opinions in this field tend to be based more on the wish than the experimental fact. The clearly controlled study made by Widdowson (1951) is therefore all the more valuable.

In studying the effect of increased rations on orphanage children living on the poor diet available in Germany in 1948 she had the rare opportunity of observing the change brought about by replacement of one sister-in-charge by another. The design of the experiment was to give orphanage B a food supplement after a six months' control period and to compare the growth of the children there with those in orphanage A, which was not to be supplemented. As shown in Fig. 37, however, the result was just the reverse of what was expected; though the B children actually gained more weight than the A children during the first, unsupplemented, six months, they gained less during the second six months despite actually taking in a measured 20 per cent more calories. The reason appeared to be that at precisely the six-month mark a certain sister had been transferred from A to become head of B. She ruled the children of B with a rod of iron and frequently chose mealtimes to administer to individual children public and often unjustified rebukes, which upset all present. An exception was the group of eight favourites (squares in the figure) whom she brought with her from orphanage A. These eight always gained more weight than the others, and on being supplemented in B gained still faster. The effect on height was less than that on weight, but of the same nature. 'Better', quotes Widdowson, 'a dinner of herbs where love is than a stalled ox and hatred therewith.'

Possibly similar factors may explain in part some of the observations made on gains in height and weight in school children during term-time as opposed to holidays (though it must be emphasized that the sister's treatment of the children was really shocking and constituted a severe emotional stress not to be compared with the occasional reprimand; the occasional reprimand to one child may be a severe pressure to another, however). In certain day and boarding schools the rate of growth in height and weight has been shown to be less during term, and particularly during the second half of term, than in the holidays (Friend, 1935, Allan, 1937, 1939, Friend and Bransby, 1947). Schools differ in this respect. In two out of three private boarding schools investigated boys aged 13 to 16 had term-time gains in height and weight which were only half as much as the holiday gains; but in the third school term and holiday gains were

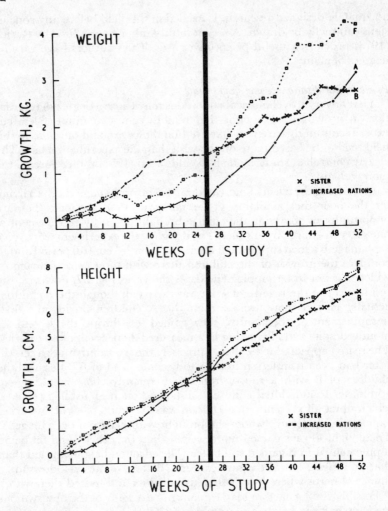

Fig. 37. Influence of sister-in-charge S on growth in weight and height of orphanage children. Presence of S marked by X plots, increased rations by = =. Orphanage B diet supplemented at time indicated by vertical bar, but sister simultaneously transferred to B (---) from A (____). Note that magnitude of growth follows presence or absence of sister, not amount of rations. Top curves (□...□) are for 8 favourites of sister, transferred with her to B from A. Redrawn from Widdowson (1951). (From Tanner, *Growth at Adolescence*, Blackwell: Oxford.)

equal (Widdowson and McCance, 1944).

These comparisons seem to be independent of seasonal effects. Many criticisms could be levelled at the techniques, especially for measuring height, used in the older investigations where very small increments are being studied. Many alternative explanations, nutritional and other, could be found for the results. Nevertheless, the subject is of potential importance and some further careful and more detailed studies—distinguishing bone, muscle and fat growth, for example, instead of lumping them all together as body weight—would provide educational authorities with valuable data on various aspects of the schools concerned. Such relatively small, though not unimportant effects must be distinguished from a rare disorder of psychological origin, recently described. Some children, under severe stress, actually switch off their secretion of growth hormone and present all the symptoms of growth hormone deficiency (including relative fatness which distinguishes them from children who have simply been undernourished). When the stress is removed the secretion of growth hormone resumes again, and a catch-up occurs which is indistinguishable from the catch-up following administration of growth hormone to a child permanently deficient in it. Such children seem to resemble an older form of the 'battered baby' syndrome in that often only one child in a family is affected, whom the parents say is 'different' from the others.

Socio-economic class and numbers in the family

Children from different socio-economic levels differ in average body size at all ages, the upper groups being always larger. In most studies socio-economic status has been defined according to the father's occupation, though in recent years in Great Britain this is becoming increasingly irrelevant as an indication of standard of living and child-centredness of home, which are probably the operative factors.

The difference in height between children of the professional and managerial classes and those of unskilled labourers is currently about 3 cm at 3 years, rising to 4 or even 5 cm at adolescence. (This is approximately the equivalent of twenty years of secular trend: see next chapter.) In weight the difference is less (from 0.5 to 4 kg in most data), since the lower socio-economic class children have a greater weight for height, probably as a result of a higher intake of sugar and other carbohydrates relative to fat and protein. In the British National Child Development Survey, a nationwide sample of children consisting of all those born in the first week of March 1958, an overall difference of 3.3 cm was found between 7-year-old children of managerial and unskilled labouring fathers (Fig. 38). Some of this difference is due to a faster tempo of growth in the well-off. But some persists into adult life, as Schreider (1964) and others have shown.

These differences are compounded by differences in height and tempo according to number of siblings in the family (Fig. 38). As one might expect, first-born children are somewhat taller than later-born children with the same number of siblings, since they have had a period of being an only child. Thus the effects of being a later-born child (for given age of mother) and of having younger siblings summate. The more mouths to feed, it seems, or simply children to look after, the slower the children

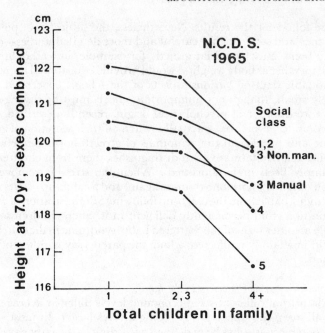

Fig. 38. Height of seven-year-old children (sexes combined) according to number of children in family and occupation (social class) of father. (Data from National Child Development Survey reported by Goldstein, 1971.)

grow. This difference is one solely of tempo, for brothers do not differ systematically according to birth order when they are fully grown. In the National Child Development Survey data about half of the social class difference persisted even when the number of siblings was allowed for.

The one exception to this occupational class gradient in children's heights is constituted by the most recent data from Sweden, published in 1976 by Dr Gunilla Lindgren of the School of Education in Stockholm. In a survey of children in all urban areas of Sweden (though not, unfortunately, in rural ones) no difference according to father's occupation was found, either of height at a given age (between 7 and 17) or in age at menarche. In agreement with this, no difference in height according to father's occupation can now be demonstrated in Swedish men conscripted for military service. Perhaps children's growth provides a meaningful measure of the classlessness of society, if that famous phrase is defined in functional rather than rhetorical terms.

CHAPTER SEVEN

The Secular Trend toward Earlier Maturity

During approximately the last hundred years in industrialized countries, and recently in some developing ones, there has been a striking tendency for the time of adolescence to become earlier, and for the whole process of growth to speed up. Thus, children born in the 1930s, for example, were considerably larger at all ages than those born in the 1900s. The change seems chiefly or entirely to be one of body size rather than of proportion or build.

The magnitude of this trend is very considerable and quite dwarfs the differences between socio-economic classes. In Fig. 39 are plotted the heights of Swedish school children measured in 1883, 1938 and 1968 (actually 1965-71). At all ages from 7 onwards the 1938 children are larger than their 1883 counterparts. The size difference amounts to about one and a half years' advance, which accords well with the advance in the age of menarche recorded over the same secular period (see below). Differences between 1938 and 1968 are much less.

British, Scandinavian and North American data all give secular trends of very similar magnitude. The average gain between 1880 and 1950 is about 1 cm and 0.5 kg per decade at ages 5 to 7; it increases to about 2 cm and 2 kg per decade during adolescence, and decreases to a figure of about 1 cm per decade for the fully grown adult. The rather scanty pre-school-age data indicate that the trend starts at birth and relative to absolute size is probably actually greater between 2 and 5 than subsequently. At least in Britain the trend started a considerable time ago, because Roberts, a factory doctor writing in 1876, said, 'A factory child of the present day at the age of nine years weighs as much as one of 10 years did in 1833 . . . each age has gained one year in forty.' In 1833, the first relatively large-scale measurement of children took place to provide parliamentary evidence used in discussion of the Factory Acts. At the time working boys aged 10 years averaged 121 cm in height compared with 140 cm today; those aged 18 years averaged 160 cm compared with 175 cm today. These differences are actually a good deal larger than the

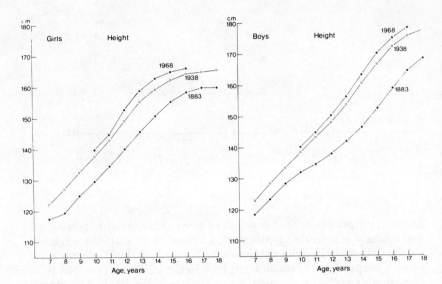

Fig. 39. Secular trend in growth of height—Swedish boys and girls measured in 1883 (Key, 1885), 1938-39 (Broman *et al.*, 1942) and 1965-71 (Lindgren, 1973). (From Ljung *et al.*, 1974.)

differences seen at present between urban slum-dwelling children in the underdeveloped countries and the affluent children of the industrialized West (see Fig. 40).

The trend in Canada, the USA, Australia and other countries has been similar. Japan shows a particularly dramatic trend. In the industrialized countries the trend is now gradually stopping, as may be seen in the Swedish data. Amongst American families with sons educated at Harvard University in successive generations the increase in height was 2.6 cm between the first two generations recorded (mean birthdates 1858 and 1888), 1.1 cm between the second pair of generations (mean birthdates 1888 and 1918) and nil between the third pair of generations (mean birthdates 1918 and 1941). In poorer sections of the community, however, the trend continues (Damon, 1968).

Better nutrition and generally improved environmental circumstances are usually given the credit, and with considerable reason. But in Britain the increase has by no means been confined to the less-well-off classes, as might be expected on a simple dietary hypothesis. Among the first schools to provide statistics on the heights of its pupils was Marlborough College, where in 1873 Fergus, the medical officer, and Rodwell, the natural science master, measured some 500 boys. Francis Galton reported their results (Galton, 1874) to the Royal Anthropological Institute; the height of the boys at 16.5 years averaged 65.5 in. Exactly 80 years later, in 1953, Marlborough College boys of 16.5 years averaged 69.6 in. in height

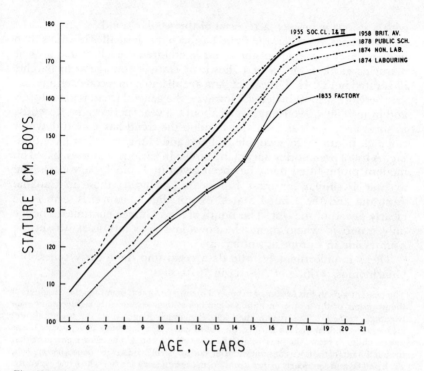

Fig. 40. Height of English boys 1833-1958 to show secular trend. 1833 factory boys, from Cowell, quoted in Bowditch (1877); 1847 labouring and non-labouring classes; 1878 'Public' school (upper classes) from Roberts (1874, 1876, 1878), Fergus and Rodwell (1874), Galton (1874); 1955 social class I and II from Birmingham Survey (Clements, unpublished); 1958 British average from Tanner (1958a). (From Tanner, *Growth at Adolescence*, Blackwell: Oxford.)

(Boyne, 1960), a gain of 4.1 in., or rather more than ½ in./decade. Despite the fact that these boys have always been drawn from the relatively well-off professional classes, their gain is between two-thirds and three-quarters of the gain made by the general population of the same age during this time. The trend toward earlier completion of growth and greater adult stature continued in the Marlbourgh College records of the 1940s and 1950s.

During the same period there has been an upward trend in adult height but only to the lesser degree of about 1 cm/decade since 1880. An astonishing series of Norwegian growth data stretching back to 1741 (Kiil, 1939) indicates little if any increase in mean male height from 1790 to 1830 and these and other data show a trend of some 0.3cm/decade in several countries from 1830 to 1880, depending on their situation *vis-à-vis* the progress of the industrial revolution. As Dr van Wieringen of Utrecht University has shown in analysing the data on height of Dutch conscripts from 1851 to the present, periods of economic setback were associated with a stoppage or even a reversal of the secular trend.

At all times, however, the trend has been much smaller in adults than in children. Thus much of the trend in children's height is due to their maturing earlier. This is best shown by statistics on age at menarche, illustrated in Fig. 41. The earlier data are all based on recollected age and are therefore suspect in detail. However, the general trend is plain to see, and from 1880 to 1960 it averaged about 0.3 years per decade. Recently, in some areas such as Oslo and London the trend has slowed down or stopped. In others, for example Holland and Hungary, it is still continuing. A list of present-day ages of menarche in various countries, based on modern probit-fitted data, has been given in Table 4 (page 101). The average is similar for most Europeans, including those in Canada, Australia and the United States, except that Italian girls seem to be clearly ahead of the rest. The Bundi of New Guinea continue to be the only group in whom menarche nowadays is as late as it was in the countryside in Europe a century ago.

There is unfortunately little data regarding these early times, but Guarinonius, writing of Austria in 1610, says:

The peasant girls in this *Landschaft* in general menstruate much later than the daughters of the townsfolk or the aristocracy, and seldom before their seventeenth, eighteenth or even twentieth year. For this reason they also live much longer than the townsfolk and aristocratic children and do not become old so early. The townsfolk have usually borne several children before the peasant girls have yet menstruated. The cause seems to be that the inhabitants of the town consume more fat food and drink and so their bodies become soft, weak and fat and come early to menstruation, in the same way as a tree which one waters too early produces earlier but less well-formed fruit than another.

Passing by Guarinonius's ruro-humoral prejudices, we may conclude that in towns menarche was expected around 14 or 15. In Manchester, England, about 1820 (at which time living standards, lowered by the beginnings of the industrial revolution, were just about at their worst) the mean menarcheal age was said to have been 14.6 years for 'educated ladies' and 15.7 for 'working women'. Since the descendants of both would now expect menarche on average at 13.0 to 13.4, the trend in the better-off classes has been about half that in the worse-off.

The causes of the trend to earlier maturity are probably multiple, though better nutrition is clearly the major factor, and perhaps in particular an increase in protein and calories in early infancy. A lessening of disease in childhood may also have contributed. Some authors have put forward the rather fanciful idea that increased psychosexual stimulation consequent on modern urban living has contributed, but there is no positive evidence for this. Girls in single-sex schools have been studiously compared with girls in co-educational schools in Finland and Sweden, with totally negative results, though whether this is a fair test of differences in psychosexual stimulation may be open to discussion. Climatic changes have also been suggested. It is true that the world mean temperature rose to about 1940 and shows signs of reversing since then.

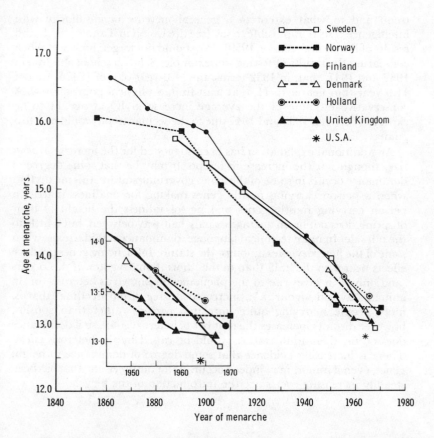

Fig. 41. Secular trend in age at menarche 1840–1970 in various countries. Values are plotted at year in which the average menarche took place. Sources of data are given in Tanner (1962 and 1973)

However, climate seems to exert at most a very minor effect, for James *et al.* (1973) have shown that descendants of Italian immigrants in Sydney have the same earlier menarche compared with descendants of Northern Europeans also in Sydney as they do in Europe. At all events, the secular trend, both in earlier maturation and in greater size is a considerable phenomenon of human biology and has, into the bargain, a host of medical, educational and sociological consequences.

It would be reasonable to infer that the brain also, though to a much smaller extent, has shown a secular trend in its speed of development and that we should therefore expect children to pass intelligence test items somewhat earlier now than previously. The average IQ of children, according to most surveys, has been either rising or else stationary, in a situation where on genetical grounds we might well have expected it to drop. To what extent we should ascribe the rise to the action of the secular trend and to what extent to a general increase in familiarity with intelligence tests is impossible to say (see discussion in Tanner, 1962, and results of Boyne and Clarke, 1959). We should not forget, however, when comparing the results of testing, for example, Scottish school children in 1932 and 1947, that, in 1932 terms, the 11.0-year-olds of 1947 were not 11.0 years but nearer to 11.5, at least from a physical point of view. A conservative estimate of the average increase in IQ at age 11 to be expected between 1932 and 1947 due to the secular trend would be 2 to 3 points.

An additional explanation has been suggested for the increase in *adult* size, though not the increase in tempo. It may be that some degree of dominance occurs in some of the genes governing stature; this means that when a person carrying mostly genes making for smallness marries a person carrying mostly genes making for tallness the height of their offspring does not lie on average exactly half-way between, but a little to the tall side. In more technical language, dominance is said to exist when some of the heterozygotes amongst the stature-influencing genes produce effects nearer to the 'tall' than to the 'short' homozygotes. If this occurs (and only if) it gives rise to the phenomenon known as heterosis (or, in animals, hybrid vigour). An increased degree of outbreeding (that is, more people marrying quite unrelated persons rather than cousins, however distant) increases the number of heterozygotes, so if dominance does occur, then adult stature would be raised by the heterosis effect. There is increasing evidence that some degree of dominance in height genes, even if minor, may indeed occur. As for outbreeding, that has been steadily increasing ever since the introduction of the bicycle.

CHAPTER EIGHT

Implications for Educational Practice and Policy

In this final chapter the implications for education of the facts of physical growth and development will be summarized. Many have been indicated in the relevant chapters, but it may be helpful to collect them together here. Many more will have occurred, no doubt, to the teacher reading this book. Only teachers themselves can find out and develop the full implications for education of these findings on physical growth. A better, if more catchpenny, title for this chapter would be 'Questions teachers should ask themselves'.

Individual differences in rate of maturing

Children differ widely in their rate of physical maturation. This is true of their growth in height and weight, of the development of the nervous structures underlying the ability to walk or to control micturition, of the time at which their endocrine glands bring about the changes of adolescence, and in all probability of the development of the brain. At adolescence, particularly, large differences exist between children of the same chronological age: one boy of 14 will be totally prepubescent, another nearly adult. There is reason to suppose that advancement in physical development (as represented by skeletal age) is associated not closely but still significantly with advancement in mental ability. It is certainly associated with emotional and behavioural differences.

The extend of this variability is considerable. The normal range of age over which menarche, the first menstrual period, may occur is from 10 to 16. Most of this variability is biological and hereditary in origin. Low living standards and poor nutrition retard development, but even if everybody lived under optimal conditions there is reason to suppose that the normal range would be reduced by less than a year.

Thus there are no social steps by which we can significantly reduce the range of individual differences in speed of physical maturation. It therefore behoves us to fit our educational system, in theory and in practice, to these biological facts.

Close linkage of chronological age and the class in which the child is placed may be considered objectionable on two grounds, when examined from this point of view. The first and minor objection comes from the relation between physical maturity and intellectual advancement. A fast-maturing boy will have a somewhat greater chance of passing any age-bound examination than will a slow-maturing boy of the same chronological age, even if the examination succeeds in testing abilities largely independent of social and emotional attitudes. To be fair, either some estimate of developmental age should be made and this factor allowed for, or else, more practically, a series of opportunities for the late maturer to use to catch up should be provided. It is no good his increasing his intellectual capacity at a time when there is nobody there, so to speak, to see him. If the usual 'bus has left by the time he arrives others should be following after.

The second and major objection comes from the relation between physical maturing and emotional and social behaviour. The needs and interests of a mature 14-year-old are totally different from those of an immature 14-year-old, and mixing them together in class or in the gymnasium obviously creates difficulties.

One might argue therefore that classes should be organized either according to strict level of attainment or according to a criterion of developmental age. If chronological age is objectionable as a criterion, what of intellectual 'age' or social 'age'? Either would produce greater homogeneity than does chronological age, though of a different sort in each instance. To what extent, if any at all, such homogeneity is advisable is a matter debated by educationists. There is something to be said for having all levels of intellectual and social capacity represented in a single class, and something to be said for having as narrow a band of each as possible. In some subjects, for example physical education, it is tolerably clear that developmental homogeneity should be aimed at, for it is manifestly unfair to pit prepubescent pupils in competitive games against postpubescents of the same age. Either the competition must be between physiological equals, or else restricted to each individual competing against his own earlier achievements. But if in relation to general school work we agree that some middle way between the two extremes is desirable, allowing a limited variety in each class, then the teacher must be prepared to face and handle an extremely complex situation.

The differences in behaviour between the physically advanced and the physically retarded of the same age are well known to every teacher; and every teacher of ability intuitively distinguishes them in his individual handling of the child. But a statement of the clear and unequivocal facts of physical growth may help him to make more conscious the basis of his distinction and to clarify the occasional misunderstanding and mistake. The teacher should be particularly aware of the needs of the excessively late developer and the excessively early one; both feel estranged from the general group of children. The isolation of the late developer continues longer and seems more often to produce effects on behaviour. This is perhaps particularly true in boys, who may substitute a false aggressive rowdiness for the genuine manly drive they see developing in their contemporaries. When at last their puberty starts, the rowdiness may rapidly subside. While present it may superficially simulate the real fed-up aggression of the mature muscular early-maturing boy longing for physical risk and the exercise of daring and strength, committed instead to sit at a desk or a machine or a printing press, performing, to him, nonsensical tricks or dully repetitive work. With reflection on the facts of physical growth the differentiation between these two types of behaviour becomes easier.

In a similar way the apparently inexplicable embarrassments of the girl who menstruates earlier than anyone else in her class, or whose breasts grow large while those of the remainder are still prepubertal, may be understood. The early-maturing boy, in general, is more likely than the late-maturing to achieve an advantageous position in school, to assume leadership in games and class activities. The same is not true, or is true to a lesser extent only, of early-maturing girls. Probably developmental status at adolescence has more significance for boys than for girls, because of the more extensive changes that adolescence brings about in them. In the complex personality of the child the effects of advancement or delay are only one of many ingredients, but they are one, and being conscious of them helps in understanding individual children. These effects are already operative in nursery school: the early-maturing child tends to be ahead of the others in motor skills and hence to have a degree of social advantage.

The effects of the secular trend must also be borne in mind, not only at adolescence but during the whole of the educational period from the nursery school onwards. Equipment and techniques suitable for the 4-year-old of thirty years ago are more suitable for the $3\frac{1}{2}$-year-old now; where they were once an impetus to advance they may now, unless continually revised, be an impediment. The present-day 14-year-old *is*, in physique and very probably in brain maturity also, the 15-year-old of a generation ago, and he must be treated accordingly. It is true he has had a year less education, and a year less experience of the world, but assimilation of experience and instruction is not measured by the calendar. If his social behaviour seems less rather than more mature (in the sense here of adult-like) that must be laid at the door of the social and educational pressures bearing or failing to bear upon him. Perhaps recognition of the effects of the secular trend would in itself help to make the approach of an older generation more acceptable to a younger one.

The question of school-leaving age

The biological variability in rate of maturing is a stumbling block in all discussions of school-leaving age. Suppose, reasonably enough, that it is at least desirable to keep children in school until puberty is completed, so that boys entering industry shall have their adult strength and endurance, and be over the more obvious effects of the adolescent worries about physical development and sexual function described in Chapter 3. This desideratum could be met by a school-leaving age of 17. But suppose, with equal reason, that a school atmosphere is not the most suitable place for some children—particularly those more suited to practical pursuits and less to the manipulation of abstract symbols and concepts—for several years after puberty is finished; after, in fact, they are adults. By this criterion a school-leaving age of 16 or 17 is undesirably late for those whose interests cannot be engaged by a 'sixth form' type of approach.

The only solution to this dilemma seems to be to get rid of the idea of a school-leaving age as such. Such a static conception can never accommodate biological material; it needs to be replaced by a more dynamic and flexible system. We need not a production-line like an apple-sorter, with children falling off at age-given points of 16 to 18, some immature and some rotted by boredom and the stultifying effect of a situation they feel intuitively to be contrived. A network rather should be the model, with many paths through it, offering to the individual child a route more in accordance with his own particular speed of development and his own particular gifts. Such a system could be built if the barriers between school and industrial community were progressively removed, so that one child went to his apprenticeship as another to a new form. In neither case would the progression be dependent on chronological age, but on physical development, emotional needs, manual capabilities and intelligence. One boy might begin to spend a considerable proportion of his time in an engineering shop from age 13 onwards, though always under the ultimate control of the educational authorities. If at 16 he had after all discovered a talent for figures, he could increase the proportion of time in the schoolroom. Another late-maturing though not very intelligent boy might remain in the more protected school environment till 16 or even 17, emerging gradually into the community as science, humanism and common sense alike dictate, and not at the occurrence of an arbitrary birthday. School-leaving age could be abolished, but 'education' continued for all up to 18 or 20. The economic system would have to be arranged so that passage from school to industry or vice versa did not penalize the child financially. The lad working in industry should, for psychological reasons, be paid for his work provided it is satisfactory; there is no proper reason why the lad remaining at school should not be equally paid, by an extension downwards of the present system of grants to university students. Doubtless the administrative difficulties of establishing such a network would be great; but that is a challenge, not an argument.

Growth and development of the nervous system

Clearly the way in which we teach children and the times at which we teach them various things must be governed by the manner of growth of their nervous systems. Of the several points stressed in the chapter on the development of the brain perhaps two require the chief emphasis. These are the concepts of maturation and of sequence.

In early childhood it is useless to begin toilet training at an age before the nervous pathways from brain to bladder are mature and functional. (It may indeed be reprehensible and in some cases it is certainly savage; but at all events it is foolish.) How often do we commit the same blunder in a more subtle form, later, during the school years? We enter here the domain of hypothesis, for we do not know to what extent the later cerebral mechanisms simply mature irrespective of environmental pressure, and to what extent each particular one is responsive to and can be influenced by attempts to learn. The hypothalamic centre controlling the time at which puberty begins, matures, simply; there is little evidence that environmental stimulation of the nervous system has much effect upon it. But the 'mental structures', as Piaget and Inhelder call them, responsible for formal intellectual operations, to what extent are they also independent of learning?

Furthermore, if we attempt to teach something too soon, what exactly happens? Do we build up cell assemblies of a sort that may prevent the creation of the optimal cell assemblies for that particular skill at the time when the child's nervous system is ready to encompass it? Conversely, if we delay too long the introduction of notions for which the child is ready, do we equally prejudice their accurate reception later? This is the question of sequence in development, of the growth gradients described in Chapter 4. The brain, no less than the limbs or the muscles or the ossification centres of the wrist, has its innate sequence of development. The sequence may differ from one child to another, but we may suppose that in each child it is largely genetically determined. Ideally as each level of brain development is reached, so the external environment should provide the data necessary for its exercise. McGraw makes the point that the young child exhibits a great urge to exercise constantly a newly acquired motor function. As the baby masters the new activity the frequency of its exercise diminishes. There is no reason to suppose that later and more complex skills involve a radical change in this desired pattern. What happens if at the moment when a skill or a 'mental structure' first develops the child is starved of exercise for it? This is the problem of the critical period also discussed in Chapter 4. Does the optimal development of each phase of the sequence of brain maturation require environmental stimulation? What happens when a part of the sequence remains unstimulated? There is some evidence that subsequent learning, not only of that skill but of others too, may be lowered in efficiency. Delay in teaching, no less than precocity, may have undesirable effects.

One may say, of course, that the times when we introduce children to particular subjects such as arithmetic, reading or algebra cannot be far wrong, because they have been established by trial and error and must reflect at least the situation of the average child. Leaving aside here the implication of the secular trend, we may admit this. But the problem of individual differences in sequence and rate of maturation obstinately remains. At present we have no psychological tests of readiness to learn such-and-such. Nor do we have any physiological tests from which we may infer that certain cell assemblies are mature and ready to receive and operate upon data of a particular sort. Undoubtedly both will come in time. But until then, and perhaps beyond, the teacher must endeavour to distinguish in the individual child a genuine readiness to embrace a particular set of concepts, and he must distinguish its first flicker, if it is to be coaxed to a steady, practised flame.

Bibliography

ABERNETHY, E. M. (1936). Relationships between mental and physical growth. *Monogr. Soc. Res. Child Developm.*, *1*, No. 7, 80 pp.

ALLAN, J. (1937). Influence of school routine on the growth and health of children. *Lancet*, *1*, 674-5.

ALLAN, J. (1939). Growth of children in day schools. *Lancet*, *1*, 1300-1.

BAYLEY, N. (1954). Some increasing parent-child similarities during the growth of children. *J. educ. Psychol.*, *45*, 1-21.

BAYLEY, N. (1956). Individual patterns of development. *Child Developm.*, *27*, 45-74.

BAYLEY, N. and PINNEAU, S. R. (1952). Tables for predicting adult heights from skeletal age: revised for use with the Greulich-Pyle hand standards. *J. Pediat.*, *40*, 423-41. (Erratum corrected in *J. Pediat.*, *41*, 371.)

BINNING, G. (1958). Earlier physical and mental maturity among Saskatoon public school children. *Canad. J. publ. Hlth.*, *49*, 9-17.

BINNING, G. (1959). The psychosomatic somatopsychic nature of school child growth. *Arch. Pediat.*, *76*, 269-81.

BOAS, F. (1941). The relation between physical and mental development. *Science*, *93*, 339-42.

BOYNE, A. W. (1960). Secular changes in the stature of adults and the growth of children, with special reference to changes in intelligence of 11-year-olds. In: *Human Growth*, Ed. J. M. Tanner. *Sym. Soc. Hum. Biol.*, Vol. 3. London: Pergamon.

BOYNE, A. W. and CLARK, J. R. (1959). Secular change in the intelligence of 11-year-old Aberdeen school children. *Hum. Biol.*, *31*, 325-33.

BROWN, J. W. (1956). The development of the nucleus of the spinal tract of V in human fetuses of 14 to 21 weeks of menstrual age. *J. comp. Neurol.*, *106*, 393-423.

BROWN, J. W. (1958). The development of subnucleus caudalis of the nucleus of the spinal tract of V. *J. comp. Neurol.*, *110*, 105-33.

127

CAMPBELL, R. V. D. and WEECH, A. A. (1941). Measures which characterize the individual during the development of behaviour in early life. *Child Developm.*, *12*, 217–36.

CHEEK, D. B. (1975). *Fetal and postnatal cellular growth.* New York: Wiley.

CLIQUET, R. L. (1968). Social mobility and the anthropological structure of populations. *Hum. Biol.*, *40*, 17–43.

CONEL, J. L. (1939). *The postnatal development of the human cerebral cortex. Vol. I. The cortex of the newborn.* Cambridge, Mass.: Harvard University Press.

CONEL, J. L. (1941). *The postnatal development of the human cerebral cortex. Vol. II. The cortex of the one-month infant.* Cambridge, Mass.: Harvard University Press.

CONEL, J. L. (1947). *The postnatal development of the human cerebral cortex. Vol. III. The cortex of the three-month infant.* Cambridge, Mass.: Harvard University Press.

CONEL, J. L. (1951). *The postnatal development of the human cerebral cortex. Vol. IV. The cortex of the six-month infant.* Cambridge, Mass.: Harvard University Press.

CONEL, J. L. (1955). *The postnatal development of the human cerebral cortex. Vol. V. The cortex of the fifteen-month infant.* Cambridge, Mass.: Harvard University Press.

CONEL, J. L. (1959). *The postnatal development of the human cerebral cortex. Vol. VI. The cortex of the twenty-four-month infant.* Cambridge, Mass.: Harvard University Press.

CONEL, J. L. (1963). *The postnatal development of the human cerebral cortex. Vol. VII. The cortex of the four-year-old child.* Cambridge, Mass.: Harvard University Press.

CONEL, J. L. (1967). *The postnatal development of the human cerebral cortex. Vol. VIII. The cortex of the six-year-old child.* Cambridge, Mass.: Harvard University Press.

CRARY, D. D. and SAWIN, P. B. (1957). Morphogenetic studies of the rabbit. XVIII. Growth of ossification centres of the vertebral centra during the 21st day. *Anat. Rec.*, *127*, 131–50.

DAMON, A. (1968). Secular trend in height and weight within Old American families at Harvard 1870–1965. 1. Within twelve four-generation families. *Amer. J. phys. Anthrop.*, *29*, 45–50.

DAVIDSON, H. H. and GOTTLIEB, L. S. (1955). The emotional maturity of pre- and post-menarcheal girls. *J. genet. Psychol.*, *86*, 261–6.

DEMISCH, A. and WARTMANN, P. (1956). Calcification of the mandibular third molar and its relation to skeletal and chronological age in children. *Child Developm.*, *27*, 459–73.

DENNIS, W. (1941). Effect of pubertas praecox on the age at thich onset of walking occurs. *Amer. J. Dis. Child.*, *61*, 951–7.

Discussions on Child Development (1956–60). Vols. I–IV. Eds. J. M. Tanner and B. Inhelder. London: Tavistock Publications.

DOBBING, J. (1974). Later development of the brain and its vulnerability. In: *Scientific Basis of Paediatrics*, Eds. J.A. Davies and J. Dobbing. London: Heinemann.

DOBBING, J. and SANDS, J. (1973). Quantitative growth and development of the human brain. *Arch. Dis. Childhood*, *48*, 757-67.

DOUGLAS, J. W. B. (1956). The age at which premature children walk. *Med. Officer*, *95*, 33-5.

DOUGLAS, J. W. B. (1960). Communication to Soc. Study Hum. Biol.

DOUGLAS, J. W. B., ROSS, J. M. and SIMPSON, H. R. (1965). The relation between height and measured educational ability in school children of the same social class, family size and stage of sexual development. *Hum. Biol.*, *37*, 178-86.

DUNN, H. L. (1921). The growth of the central nervous system in the human fetus as expressed by graphic analysis and empirical formulae. *J. comp. Neurol.*, *33*, 405-91.

EAYRS, J. T. and HORN, G. (1955). The development of the cerebral cortex in hypothyroid and starved rats. *Anat. Rec.*, *121*, 53-61.

EAYRS, J. T. and LISHMAN, W. A. (1955). The maturation of behaviour in hypothyroidism and starvation. *Brit. J. anim. Behav.*, *3*, 17-24.

ELIAS, M. and SAMONDS, K.W. (1977). Protein and calorie malnutrition in infant cebus monkeys, growth and behavioral development during deprivation and rehabilitation. *Amer. J. clin. Nutrition*, *30*, 355-66.

EVELETH, P. B. and TANNER, J. M. (1976). *World-Wide Variation in Human Growth*. London: Cambridge University Press.

FAUST, M. S. (1960). Development maturity as a determinant in prestige of adolescent girls. *Child Developm.*, *31*, 173-84.

FELTS, W. J. L. (1959). Transplantation studies of factors in skeletal organogenesis. I. The subcutaneously implanted immature long-bone of the rat and mouse. *Amer. J. phys. Anthrop.*, *N.S.*, *17*, 201-15.

FLEAGLE, J.C., SAMONDS, K.W. and HEGSTED, D. M. (1975). Physical growth of cebus monkeys, *Cebus albifrons*, during protein or calorie deficiency. *Amer. J. clin. Nutrition*, *28*, 246-53.

FRANZBLAU. R. N. (1935). Race differences in mental and physical traits: studied in different environments. *Arch. Psychol.*, No. 177.

FREEMAN, F. N. and FLORY, C. D. (1937). Growth in intellectual ability as measured by repeated tests. *Monogr. Soc. Res. Child Developm.*, *2*, No. 2.

FRIEND, G. E. (1935). *The schoolboy: a study of his nutrition, physical development and health*. Cambridge: Heffer. 128 pp.

FRIEND, G. E. and BRANSBY, E. R. (1947). Physique and growth of schoolboys. *Lancet*, *2*, 677-81.

GALTON, F. (1874). Notes on the Marlborough School statistics. *J. Anthrop. Inst. Great Britain and Ireland*, *4*, 130-5.

GOLDSTEIN, H. (1971). Factors influencing the height of seven-year-old children: Results from the National Child Development Study. *Hum. Biol. 43*, 92–111.

GREULICH, W. W. and PYLE, S. I. (1959). *Radiographic atlas of skeletal development of the hand and wrist.* Second edition. Stanford: University Press.

HALL, W. S. (1896). Changes in the proportions of the human body during the period of growth. *J. Anthrop, Inst. Great Brit. & Ireland, 25,* 21–46.

HEBB, D. O. (1949). *The organization of behavior.* New York: Wiley.

HONZIK, M. P. (1957). Development studies of parent-child resemblance in intelligence. *Child Developm., 28,* 215–28.

HOWARD, E., GRANOFF, D. and BUJNOVSKY, P. (1969). DNA, RNA and cholesterol increases in cerebrum and cerebellum during development of human fetuses. *Brain Res., 14,* 697–706.

INHELDER, B. and PIAGET, J. (1958). *The growth of logical thinking from childhood to adolescence.* London: Kegan Paul.

ISRAELSOHN, W. J. (1960). Description and modes of analysis of human growth. In: *Human Growth,* Ed. J. M. Tanner. *Sym. Soc. Hum. Biol., Vol. 3.* London: Pergamon.

JAMES, D. L., HEMPHILL, W. and MEYERS, E. S. A. (1973). *Height, weight and other physical characteristics of New South Wales children. Part 1. Children aged 5 years and over.* Sydney, New South Wales: Department of Health.

JANES, M.D. (1975). Physical and psychological growth and development of Nigerians. *Environmental Child Health, 121,* 26–30.

JENKINS, G. B. (1921). Relative weight and volume of the component parts of the brain of the human embryo at different stages of development. *Contr. Embryol. Carneg. Instn., No. 59, 13,* 41–60.

JONES, M. C. (1957). The later careers of boys who were early- or late-maturing. *Child Developm., 28,* 113–28.

JONES, M. C. and BAYLEY, N. (1950). Physical maturing among boys as related to behaviour. *J. educ. Psychol., 41,* 129–48.

JONES, M. C. and MUSSEN, P. H. (1958). Self-conceptions, motivations and interpersonal attitudes of early- and late-maturing girls. *Child Developm., 29,* 491–501.

KEENE, M. F. L. and HEWER, E. E. (1931). Some observations on myelination in the human central nervous system. *J. Anat., 66,* 1–13.

KIIL, V. (1939). Stature and growth of Norwegian men during the last 200 years. *Skrifter utgitt av det Norske Videnskaps-Akademi i Oslo. I. Mat-Naturv. Klass.* No. 6. 175 pp.

KRAUS, B. S., WISE, W. J. and FREI, R. H. (1959). Heredity and the craniofacial complex. *Amer. J. Orthodont., 45,* 172–217.

LANGWORTHY, O. R. (1933). Development of behaviour patterns and myelinization of the nervous system in the human fetus and infant. *Contrib. Embryol. Carneg. Instn., No. 139, 24,* pp. 1–57.

LINDGREN, G. (1976). Height, weight and menarche in Swedish urban school children in relation to socio-economic and regional factors. *Ann. hum. Biol., 3,* 501-28.

McGRAW, M. B. (1943). *The neuromuscular maturation of the human infant.* New York: Columbia University.

MARK, R. (1974). *Memory and nerve cell connections.* Oxford: Clarendon Press.

MARSHALL, W. A. (1971). The evaluation of growth rate in height over periods of less than one year. *Arch. Dis. Childhood, 46,* 414-20.

MARSHALL, W. A. (1974). Inter-relationships of skeletal maturation, sexual development and somatic growth in man. *Ann. hum. Biol., 1,* 29-40.

MARSHALL, W. A. and SWAN, A. V. (1971). Seasonal variation in growth rates of normal and blind children. *Hum. Biol., 43,* 502.

MARSHALL, W. A. and TANNER, J. M. (1969). Variation in the pattern of pubertal changes in girls. *Arch. Dis. Childhood, 44,* 291-303.

MARSHALL, W. A. and TANNER, J. M. (1970). Variation in the pattern of pubertal changes in boys. *Arch. Dis. Childhood, 45,* 13-23.

MEREDITH, H. V. (1939). Length of head and neck, trunk and lower extremities on Iowa City children aged 7-17 years. *Child Developm., 10,* 129-44.

MILLER, F. J. W., COURT, S. D. M., WALTON, W. S. and KNOX, E. G. (1960). *Growing up in Newcastle-upon-Tyne: a continuing study of health and illness in young children within their families,* London: Oxford University Press.

MONEY, J. and HAMPSON, J. G. (1955). Idiopathic sexual precocity in the male. *Psychosom, Med., 17,* 1-15.

MUSSEN, P. H. and JONES, M. C. (1957). Self-conceptions, motivations and interpersonal attitudes of late- and early-maturing boys. *Child Developm., 28,* 243-56.

MUSSEN, P. H. and JONES, M. C. (1958). The behaviour-inferred motivations of late- and early-maturing boys. *Child Developm., 29,* 61-7.

NOBACK, C. R. and MOSS, M. L. (1956). Differential growth of the human brain. *J. comp. Neurol., 105,* 539-51.

ODUNTAN, S.O., AYENI, O. and KALE, O.O. (1976) The age of menarche in Nigerian girls. *Ann. Hum. Biol., 3,* 269-74.

PECKHAM, C., BUTLER, N. and FREW, R. (1977). Medical and social aspects of children with educational problems. Unpublished MS.

PENFIELD, W. and RASMUSSEN, T. (1950) *The Cerebral Cortex of Man.* New York: Macmillan.

RABINOWICZ, T. (1978). The differentiate maturation of the human cerebral cortex. In: *Human Growth, Vol. 1,* Eds. F. Falkner and J. M. Tanner. New York: Plenum.

RARICK, C. L. (1973). *Physical activity, human growth and development.* New York and London: Academic Press.

RICHARDSON, S. A. (1975). Physical growth of Jamaican school children who were severely malnourished before 2 years of age. *J. biosoc. Sci., 7*, 445-62.

SCAMMON, R. E. and DUNN, H. (1924). On the growth of the human cerebellum in early life. *Proc. Soc. exp. Biol., N.Y., 21*, 217-21.

SCHIOTZ, C. (1923). Physical development of children and young people during the age of 7 to 18-20 years. An investigation of 28,700 pupils of Public (elementary) and Higher (secondary) schools in Christiania. *Videnskapsselskapets Skr. I. Mat.-Naturv. Klasse*, No. 4, 54 pp.

SCHONFELD, W. A. (1950). Deficient development of masculinity. A psychosomatic problem of adolescence. *Amer. J. Dis. Child., 79*, 17-29.

SCHREIDER, E. (1956). Taille et capacités mentales: étude experimentale et statistique d'une correlation apparemment 'simple'. *Biotypol., 17*, 21-37.

SCHREIDER, E. (1964). Recherches sur la stratification sociale des caractères biologiques. *Biotypologie, 25*, 105-35.

SCHULTZ, D. M., GORDIANO, D. A. and SCHULTZ, D. H. (1962). Weights of organs of fetuses and infants. *Arch. Pathology, 74*, 244-50.

SCOTT, E. M., ILLSLEY, R. and THOMSON, A. M. (1956). A psychological investigation of primigravidae. II. Maternal social class, age, physique and intelligence. *J. Obstet. Gynaec. Brit. Emp., 63*, 338-43.

SCOTT, J. A. (1961). *Report on the heights and weights (and other measurements) of school pupils in the County of London in 1959.* London: County Council.

SCOTT, J. A. (1962). Intelligence, physique and family size. *Brit. J. prev. Soc. Med., 16*, 165-73.

SCOTTISH COUNCIL FOR RESEARCH IN EDUCATION (1953). *Social implications of the 1947 Scottish Mental Survey.* London: University of London Press.

SHOLL, D. A. (1956). *The organization of the cerebral cortex.* London: Methuen.

SHUTTLEWORTH, F. K. (1937). The physical and mental growth of girls and boys age six to nineteen in relation to age at maximum growth. *Monogr. Soc. Res. Child Developm., 4*, No. 3.

SONTAG, L. W., BAKER, C. T. and NELSON, V. L. (1958). Mental growth and personality development: a longitudinal study. *Monogr. Soc. Res. Child Developm., 23*, No. 2.

STEIN, Z., SUSSER, M., SAENGER, G. and MAROLLA, F. (1975). *Famine and human development: the Dutch hunger winter of 1944-1945.* New York: Oxford University Press.

STONE, C. P. and BARKER, R. G. (1937). Aspects of personality and intelligence in post-menarcheal girls and pre-menarcheal girls of the same chronological ages. *J. comp. physiol. Psychol., 23*, 439-55.

STONE, C. P. and BARKER, R. G. (1939). The attitudes and interests of pre-menarcheal and post-menarcheal girls. *J. genet. Psychol.*, *54*, 27-71.

SUSANNE, C. (1975). Genetic and environmental influence on morphological characteristics. *Ann. hum. Biol.*, *2*, 279-88.

TANNER, J. M. (1952). The effect of weight-training on physique. *Amer. J. phys. Anthrop.*, *N.S.*, *10*, 427-62.

TANNER, J. M. (1960). The genetics of growth. In *Human Growth*. Ed. J. M. Tanner. *Sym. Soc. Hum. Biol.*, *Vol. 3*. London: Pergamon.

TANNER, J. M. (1962). *Growth at adolescence*. Second edition. Oxford: Blackwell.

TANNER, J. M. (1964). *The Physique of the Olympic Athlete*. London: Allen and Unwin, 126 pp. Distributed by Institute of Child Health, University of London.

TANNER, J. M. (1966). Galtonian Eugenics and the study of growth. The relation of body size, intelligence test score, and social circumstances in children and adults. *Eugen. Rev.*, *58*, 122-35. Reprinted in: *Trends and Issues in Developmental Psychology*, Eds. P. H. Mussen, J. Largen and M. Covington. New York: Holt, 1969.

TANNER, J. M. (1973). Trend towards earlier menarche in London, Oslo, Copenhagen, the Netherlands and Hungary. *Nature*, *243*, 95-6.

TANNER, J. M., (1975). Towards complete success in the treatment of growth hormone deficiency; a plea for earlier ascertainment. *Health Trends*, *7*, 61-5.

TANNER, J.M., GOLDSTEIN, H. and WHITEHOUSE, R.H. (1970). Standards for children's height at ages 2 to 9 years, allowing for height of parents. *Arch. Dis. Childhood*, *45*, 755-62.

TANNER, J. M. and INHELDER, B. (Eds.) (1956-60). *Discussions on child development*, *Vols. I-IV*. London: Tavistock Publ.

TANNER, J. M. and WHITEHOUSE, R. H. (1959a). Standards for height and weight of British children from birth to maturity. *Lancet*, *2*, 1086-8.

TANNER, J. M. and WHITEHOUSE, R. H. (1959b). Standards for skeletal maturity based on a study of 3,000 British children. London Univ. Inst. Child Health MS.

TANNER, J. M. and WHITEHOUSE, R. H. (1975). Revised standards for triceps and subscapular skinfolds in British children. *Arch. Dis. Childhood*, *50*, 142-5.

TANNER, J. M., WHITEHOUSE, R. H., MARSHALL, W. A., HEALY, M. J. R. and GOLDSTEIN, H. (1975). *Assessment of Skeletal Maturity and Prediction of Adult Height*. London: Academic Press.

THOMSON, A.M. (1959). Maternal stature and reproductive efficiency. *Eugen. Rev.*, *51*, 157-62.

TUTTENHAM, R. D. and SNYDER, M. M. (1954). Physical growth of

California boys and girls from birth to eighteen years. *Univ. Calif. Publ. Child Developm.*, *1*, 183–364.

UDJUS, L. G. (1964). *Anthropometrical changes in Norwegian men in the twentieth century.* Oslo, Universitatsforlaget.

VAN WIERINGEN, J. C. (1977). Secular growth changes. In: *Human Growth, Vol. 1,* Eds. F. Falkner and J. M. Tanner. New York: Plenum.

WADDINGTON, C. H. (1957). *The strategy of the genes.* London: Allen and Unwin.

WATERLOW, J. C. and PAYNE, P. R. (1975). The Protein gap. *Nature, 258,* 113–17.

WEISS, P. (Ed.) (1950). *Genetic neurology. Problems of the development, growth, and regeneration of the nervous system and of its functions.* Chicago: University Press.

WHITE HOUSE CONFERENCE ON CHILD HEALTH AND PRO-TECTION, SECTION I (1933). *Growth and development of the child. Part II. Anatomy and physiology.* New York: Century.

WIDDOWSON, E. M. (1951). Mental contentment and physical growth. *Lancet, 1,* 1316–18.

WIDDOWSON, E. M. and McCANCE, R. A. (1944). Growth at home and at school. *Lancet, 2,* 152–3.

WILLIER, B. H., WEISS, P. A. and HAMBURGER, V. (Eds.) (1955). *Analysis of development.* Philadelphia: Saunders.

WILSON, R. S. (1976). Concordance in physical growth for monozygotic and dizygotic twins. *Ann. hum. Biol., 3,* 1–10.

WITELSON, S. F. (1976). Sex and the single hemisphere; specialisation of the right hemisphere for spatial processing. *Science, 193,* 425–7.

YAKOVLEV, P. I. and LECOURS, A. R. (1967). The myelogenetic cycles of regional maturation of the brain. In: *Regional Development of the Brain in Early Life,* Ed. A. Minkoski. Oxford: Blackwell.

Glossary

Words in italic type are defined in this glossary

AREA, ASSOCIATION. An area of the cerebral cortex in which interpretation and integration of visual, auditory and other sensory information occurs.

AREA, MOTOR (of the cerebral cortex). The area of the cortex which is essential to control of voluntary movements. See Fig. 27.

AREA, SENSORY (of the cerebral cortex). The area of the cortex, situated in the *parietal lobes* (*q.v.* under Lobe), which is concerned with the perception of physical sensation. See Fig. 27.

AXILLARY. Pertaining to the armpit.

AXON. Defined on p. 72.

BODY, GENICULATE. Centre in the *midbrain* responsible for relaying auditory and visual information to the cerebral cortex.

BODY, LATERAL GENICULATE. Centre in the *midbrain* responsible for relaying information from the *optic tracts* to the area of the cerebral cortex concerned with vision.

BRAIN, MID. The short narrow pillar-like portion of the brain, immediately above the *pons* and *medulla*. It contains centres for relaying information to the cerebral cortex from other parts of the nervous system or for transmitting downwards the controlling influence of the cortex over the nervous system.

BUDS, TEETH. The primary outgrowths which evenutally develop into teeth.

CAUDAL. Literally, towards the tail; in man, downwards.

CELL. The smallest unit of living *tissues*, consisting of a microscopic amount of protoplasm (a watery solution of various substances vital for life, such as protein and carbohydrate) with a nucleus of slightly different material containing the *chromosomes*. AT THE CELLULAR LEVEL. In terms of the chemical changes occurring in the cells.

CENTILE. Defined on p. 36.

CEREBELLUM. Part of the brain, situated behind the *midbrain, pons* and *medulla* and connected to these by means of three bundles of nerve fibres which enable information to be conveyed to and from the cerebral cortex and *spinal cord*. The cerebellum is concerned with the smooth and even execution of voluntary movements.

CEREBRUM. The chief portion of the brain in human beings, occupying the whole upper part of the cranium, and consisting of the right and left CEREBRAL

HEMISPHERES. The most highly developed functions of the nervous system—memory, intelligence, etc.—and the centres for sight, hearing, smell, taste and general body sensations are seated in the cerebral hemispheres.

CERVICAL. At the level of the neck.

CERVICO-ROSTRAL. From the neck upwards.

CHARACTERS, SECONDARY SEX. Those characters, apart from the development of the reproductive organs, which make their appearance at *puberty*. They include the growth of *pubic* and *axillary* hair in both sexes, the bass voice and beard in men and the development of the breasts in women.

CHROMOSOMES. Strands of complex chemical material contained in the nuclei of cells. The chromosomes are responsible for the manner in which cells differentiate and for the transmission of inherited characteristics. SEX CHROMOSOMES. One particular pair of chromosomes which in the female are similar and called X and X, and in the male dissimilar and called X and Y.

CIRCUITS, REVERBERATING NERVE. Patterns of *nerve cell* activities wherein impulses are sent down the fibres of one nerve cell, passed on by another and sent on by it to, amongst others, the first again.

COEFFICIENT, CORRELATION. Defined on p. 63.

CONSERVATION, IDEA OF. The realization that in certain physical transactions the volume, mass, or energy remains unchanged. This realization is absent in young children: thus if a certain amount of water is poured from a wide glass into a narrower one, so that the level of the water is raised, a young child may say that there is more water than there was before.

CORD, SPINAL. Part of the central nervous system passing from the brain to the lower part of the back inside the vertebral column.

CORPUS CALLOSUM. A mass of *white matter* consisting of nerve fibres connecting the two *cerebral hemispheres* with each other.

CORPUS STRIATUM. A mass of *grey matter* in the brain concerned in some way with the control of muscle, and probably having a steadying influence on muscular movements.

CORTEX, OCCIPITAL. The area of the cerebral cortex devoted to vision and the interpretation of visual experience. See Fig. 27.

CORTISONE. A *hormone* similar to that produced by the adrenal cortex.

CRETIN. An individual of stunted physical and mental development as a result of a deficiency of thyroid *hormone* dating from an early age.

CURVE, GAUSSIAN. The graphic, bell-shaped representation of the *Normal distribution* such as is characteristic of the heights of a random sample of men, or the errors made in reading a physical instrument.

CYTOPLASM. The portion of the cell outside the nucleus.

DENDRITE. A process, or filament of a *nerve cell*, receiving incoming impulses.

DENTITION, DECIDUOUS. The teeth which erupt and then are lost during childhood; the primary or milk teeth.

DEVIATION, STANDARD. A measure of the dispersion of a set of values around the average or mean value, in the case of a *Gaussian curve*.

DIENCEPHALON. One of the two broad divisions of the brain that in evolutionary history differentiated from the primitive forebrain.

DIFFERENTIATION. Increase in complexity and specialization of cells and *tissues* during development.

DISTRIBUTION. The set of relative frequencies or probabilities with which various values of a variable quantity occur. A very well-known and common one is the GAUSSIAN, or NORMAL DISTRIBUTION.

DYNAMOMETER. An instrument for the measurement of muscular strength, particularly of the hand, such as a spring balance.

ELECTROENCEPHALOGRAM (EEG). A graphic record of the minute changes in electric potential associated with the functioning of the *nerve cells* of the brain, detected by means of electrodes applied to the scalp.

EMBRYO. The offspring of any species in the earliest stages of development (in human beings, during the first three months after conception).

EMBRYOLOGY. The study of the development of *embryos*.

EMISSION, SEMINAL. The ejection from the penis of fluid containing *sperm*. This occurs close to the time of the male orgasm, or sexual climax.

EPIPHYSES. Areas found at the ends of most bones, which ossify separately from the greater part of the bone: growth of long bones take place between the epiphysis and the main bone.

ERROR, SAMPLING (e.g. of the mean). The discrepancy between a numerical value calculated from a sample, and the same value calculated from the population from which the sample was drawn. This discrepancy tends to decrease as the size of the sample increases.

EXTENSOR. A muscle which on contraction causes a limb to extend or straighten.

FETUS. The offspring of mammals during the later stages of prenatal development (in human beings, during the six months immediately preceding birth). FETAL LIFE refers to this period of development.

FLEXOR. A muscle which on contraction causes a limb to flex or bend.

GANGLIA, BASAL. A mass of *grey matter* lying below the cerebral cortex and including the *corpus striatum*. This part of the brain is mainly concerned with the maintenance of posture.

GENES. Ultra-microscopic particles which are situated on the *chromosomes* and which are the agents for the transmission of hereditary characteristics.

GENITALIA. The reproductive organs, male and female.

GLAND, ENDOCRINE. An organ which produces and discharges directly into the blood-stream a substance (a *hormone*) which is thus carried to the various *tissues* of the body upon which it exerts an effect.

GLAND, PITUITARY. The *endocrine gland* situated in the head (see p. 28) which exerts an overall control of the functioning of most other endocrine glands of the body. It also secretes a *hormone* controlling growth.

GLANDS, ADRENAL. A pair of *endocrine glands*, situated immediately above the kidneys, each consisting of an inner portion, the *medulla*, which secretes the *hormone* adrenaline, and an outer portion, the cortex, which secretes a number of hormones exerting a controlling influence over several body functions.

HAEMOGLOBIN. The protein in red blood cells which is responsible for carrying oxygen from the lungs to the *tissues* where it is utilized in *metabolic* processes. The haemoglobin is responsible for the red colour of these cells.

HISTOLOGY. The study of the cells of living *tissues*.

HORMONE. A substance discharged by an *endocrine gland* into the blood and carried to various sites in the body where it influences the functional activity, or the growth and development of *tissues*.

HORMONES, STEROID. Defined on p. 27. Several steroid hormones are produced by the *adrenal gland*.

HYDROCORTISONE. A *hormone* produced by the *adrenal gland*.

HYPOTHALAMUS. Defined on p. 29.

LARYNX. The organ, situated in the neck, which contains the vocal cords and is responsible for voice production.

LOBE, FRONTAL. The area of the cerebral cortex, at the front of the brain, which includes the motor cortex, but also a large area of which little is definitely known. See Fig. 27.

LOBE, OCCIPITAL. The area of the cerebral cortex concerned with vision. See Fig. 27.

LOBE, PARIETAL. The area of the cerebral cortex where sensations of touch, warmth and coolness, and of muscular movements are interpreted. See Fig. 27.

LOBE, TEMPORAL. The area of the cerebral cortex where sound is perceived and interpreted. See Fig. 27.

MASTURBATION. Self-manipulation of the *genitalia* in order to obtain pleasurable sensations, generally leading to a climax (or orgasm).

MATTER, GREY. *Nerve cells,* constituting the outer portion of the brain and the inner portion of the *spinal cord.*

MATTER, WHITE. Nerve fibres constituting the central mass of the brain and the outer portion of the *spinal cord.*

MEAN. Average, obtained by adding up a set of values and dividing the sum by the number of values counted.

MEDIAN. The value of the middle individual, when all the individuals are arranged in increasing order of the variable under discussion.

MEDULLA, OBLONGATA. The continuation upwards of the spinal cord in the brain. The portion between *spinal cord* and *pons.*

METABOLISM. A general term applied to the various chemical processes taking place in living *tissues,* e.g., the oxidation of food materials, with the consequent liberation of energy.

MICTURITION. The voiding of urine.

MIDBRAIN. *See* BRAIN, MID.

MYELIN. A white fat-like substance. The majority of nerves in the central nervous system are ensheathed by this substance, which acts somewhat after the manner of an insulator.

MYELINATION. The acquisition by a nerve of a *myelin* sheath.

MYOPIA. Shortsightedness; due to the lens of the eye being too powerful in relation to the shape of the eye, so that light rays are brought to a focus in front of, instead of on, the *retina.*

NEONATAL. Immediately following birth.

NERVE, THIRD. The oculomotor nerve, running from the brain to the eye muscles.

NERVE, FIFTH. A group of nerve fibres ascending to and descending from the cerebral cortex permitting discrimination between fine sensations of touch. Nerve fibres conveying information concerning painful sensations in the face and controlling the muscles used in chewing are included in this group of nerves.

NEUROFIBRIL. Defined on p. 73. Fine fibrils common to all *nerve cells,* which are only apparent after the nerve cell has been stained in a particular way.

NEUROGLIA. The neuroglia, or NEUROGLIAL CELLS, are cells which form a supporting framework for the nervous elements proper.

NEURON OR NERVE CELL. The structural unit of the nervous system. It consists of a cell body and one or more processes, or filaments (*axons* and *dendrites*) constituting the nerve fibres. The axon transmits information from the cell body to the cell body or dendrites of another cell, or to a muscle, while the dendrites, which may be branched, convey information to the cell body.

NUCLEUS, DENTATE. A mass of *grey matter* in the *cerebellum*.

OSSIFICATION. The conversion of cartilage to bone.

OVARIES. The organs which form the germ cells, or *ova*, in the female.

OVUM (plural OVA). The germ cells which are produced by the *ovaries*. The penetration of an *ovum* by a *sperm* (fertilization), as a result of coitus, leads to pregnancy.

PATHOLOGICAL. Resulting from disease.

PATTERNS, DOMAIN. Patterns of activity displayed by *nerve cells* in the cerebral cortex.

PERCENTILE. See *centile*.

PERIOD, SENSITIVE. Defined on p. 13 and p. 55.

PONS. A part of the brain situated immediately above the *medulla*, relaying information from the cerebral cortex and the *midbrain* to the *spinal cord* and *cerebellum*.

POSTMENARCHEAL. After the first menstrual period.

POSTNATAL. After birth.

PREMENARCHEAL. Before the first menstrual period.

PRENATAL. Before birth.

PROBIT or LOGIT (transformation). Statistical techniques for summarizing sets of observations.

PSYCHOSEXUAL. Relating to the mental and emotional aspects of sex as distinct from its physical manifestations.

PUBERTY. The period of maturation of the male and female reproductive organs.

PUBIC. Relating to the pubic bone, the portion of the hip-bone forming the front of the pelvis. PUBIC HAIR is the hair which begins to grow in this region at puberty.

REACTANT. A substance taking part in a chemical reaction.

RESPONSE, REFLEX. An involuntary response to a stimulus, conscious or unconscious.

RETINA. The light-sensitive *tissue* lining the posterior wall of the eye, which in humans is shaped like a globe. Light enters the eye through the transparent anterior region and the lens, which focuses the light rays on the retina.

ROSTRAL. The head end of the body.

SCROTUM. The pouch of skin suspended from the *pubic* region of the body, containing the *testes*.

SECRETION (e.g., from the *endocrine gland*). A substance produced by gland cells and discharged by them either into the blood (endocrine secretion) (*hormones*) or to the exterior of the body, the gut, etc. (as in sweat, digestive juices).

SPERM (i.e. SPERMATOZOON). The mature male germ cell, deposited in the upper part of the vagina during coitus. It fertilizes the *ovum*.

STUDY, CROSS-SECTIONAL. Defined on p. 18.

STUDY, LONGITUDINAL. Defined on p. 19.

SUBCUTANEOUS (fat). Immediately beneath the skin.

SUBSTANCE, NISSL. Defined on p. 73.

TEETH, ERUPTION OF. The appearance of teeth through the gums.

TESTES. The male reproductive organs (corresponding to the female *ovaries*), responsible for the production of the male germ cells or *sperm*.

THALAMUS. A mass of *grey matter* in the *cerebrum,* constituting the main relay station to the cortex for sensations of temperature, touch and muscle sense.

TISSUES. Aggregations of similar cells which have differentiated to perform a certain function. Examples: nerve tissue, muscle tissue, glandular tissue.

TISSUES, LYMPHOID. Tissue which is responsible for the manufacture of cells called lymphocytes. These cells play an important part in establishing resistance to infection and in the processes of immunity.

TRACTS. OLFACTORY. Bundles of nerve fibres conveying information concerning smell to the cerebral cortex.

TRACTS, OPTIC. Bundles of nerve fibres conveying information concerning vision to the cerebral cortex.

TRACTS, PYRAMIDAL. Nerve fibres descending from the cerebral cortex (motor area) to the *spinal cord,* establishing brain control over muscles.

UTERINE. Of the womb or uterus.

VESTIBULAR SYSTEM. A group of cells in the *medulla,* relaying information from the balance-sensitive mechanism of the ear, to the *cerebellum* and the *spinal cord.* The sense of balance depends on this system.

Index

adenoids, 21, 23
adolescence
  and athletic ability, 24–5, 27, 48
  development at, 23–7, 56, 62–3,
    98
  early *v.* late maturity, 12, 32–3,
    34, 37–40, 41–9, 121–6
  hormonal changes during, 27–9
  see also secular trend
adolescent growth spurt, 15, 16–18,
  20–1, 23–7, 30, 46, 48, 64, 66,
  97
adrenal glands, 27, 40, 110, 137
androgenic hormone, 96
anorexia, *see* starvation
anxiety, psychosexual, 46–7
arm, 13, 25–6, 57–8
association areas of brain, 74, 76,
  77, 85, 135
auditory area of brain, 74, 76, 77,
  78
axons, 72–3, 74, 82, 83

basal ganglia, 69, 137
'battered babies', 113
behaviour, 11, 66, 79, 80, 109
  and developmental age, 34, 42, 45,
    123
birth order, 113–14
bladder control, 81, 86, 125
blood, 27, 29, 73
body shape, 27, 34–5, 91–2, 98
bones, growth of, 12, 16, 35–7, 54,
  99, *see also* skeletal age, skeletal
  growth

brain, 67–89 *passim*
  areas of, 74, 75
  and EEG, 67, 84–5
  growth of, 12, 13, 21–2, 42, 56, 59,
    61, 62, 68–78, 107, 125
  influences on development, 80–4
  and intelligence, 78–9, 85–9, 119
  sex differences in?, 27, 80, 81
  tumours, 84
  weight of, 68–9
breast, 29, 32, 48
  enlargement in boys, 30–1
  milk, 104, 105, 110

calf, 13, 25, 57
castration complex, 46–7
catch-up growth, 52–4, 104, 105–6,
  108–9, 110, 113
cells, 55, 72, 83, 86, 91, 135, *see also*
  neurons
cerebellum, 67, 69, 70, 71, 73, 78,
  135
cerebral cortex, 72, 73–9, 84
cerebral hemispheres, 71, 80, 136
cerebrum, 67, 69, 70, 71, 73, 135
chromosomes, 55, 56, 59, 60, 93, 136
cingulate gyrus, 74, 77
climate, effect on development,
  99–102, 118–19
cognitive development, 13, 62, 63,
  105, 125
  and brain development, 68, 78–9,
    84, 85, 86, 89
  see also intelligence, learning
connectivity, of cells, 73, 79, 82, 83, 86

corpus callosum, 69, 136
crawling, 61, 86
cretins, 81, 136
critical period, *see* sensitive period
cytoplasm, 73, 74, 92, 136

dendrites, 72-3, 74, 79, 81, 84, 86
dental age, 35, 36, 37-8, 39-40, 63,
    see also teeth
developmental age, 11, 48-9, 95, 96,
    122
  measuring, 12-13, 31, 34-6, 37,
    49, 112-13
DNA, 90, 91

ear, 21
education, 11, 14, 35, 41, 48-9,
    63-4, 111-12, 121-6
EEG, 67, 84-5, 137
embryological development, 55, 56,
    57, 91
emotional development, 62, 79, 105,
    109, 111
  and physical development, 41,
    45-9
endocrine system, 15, 27-30, 40, 56,
    60, 66, 101, 110, *see also*
    hormones
  control of, 29
environment, 13, 60, 106, 109-10,
    116
  and intellectual development, 79,
    84, 86, 89, 109, 125
  interaction with heredity, 13, 86,
    90-1, 92
  stimulation in, 79, 81, 84, 90, 125
evolution, 13, 91, 99-100, 104, 108
exercise, 23, 80, 110-11
eye, development of, 21, 22-3, 55,
    59, 101
  and brain, 82-3
  cataracts, 55
  see also vision

face, 22, 59
family size
  and growth, 113-14
  and intelligence, 44, 107
fat, *see* subcutaneous fat
fetal growth, 40, 59, 71, 78, 105, 107

fetus, 59, 65, 76n., 91, 137
finger, 27, 59
foot, 13, 57, 58
frontal lobe of brain, 74-6, 77, 138

genes, 40, 50, 59, 60, 66, 68, 90,
    92-6, 98, 120, 137
  age-limited, 66, 68, 93
  sex-limited, 93
geniculate body of brain, 82-3, 135
glial cells, 73
growth
  gradients, 11, 13, 56-9, 68, 125
  regularity of, 16, 38-9, 50-1, 63,
    82-3, 125

hair
  axillary, 30
  facial, 30
  pubic, 30-2
hand, 13, 35, 58
  grip, 25-7
head, 38, 58, 92
hearing, 77
heart, 24
height
  and adolescent spurt, 32, 46
  genetic influence on, 92, 93-6
  and intelligence, 44
  and nutrition, 104, 105, 110, 111
  predicting, 63-4, 65
  and secular trend 117-18
  velocity, 15-18, 113-14
'height age', 42
hippocampal gyrus, 74, 77
hormones, 21, 25, 27-30, 40, 56, 93,
    97-8, 101, 113, 137
  growth hormone, 29-30, 53-4, 113
  releasing hormones, 29
  sex hormones, 23, 25, 27-9, 40, 56
  see also endocrine system
hospitalization, 109, 110
Huntington's chorea, 66
hypothalamus, 29, 69

illness, effect on growth, 51, 110, 118
individual differences, 14, 86, 122, *see
    also* intelligence, personality,
    variability of growth
infant mortality, 20
insula, 74-6, 77

intelligence, 13, 36, 41-5, 78-9,
    85-9, 95, 105, 107, 109, 122
and brain development, 78-9,
    85-7, 119
and environment, 45, 79, 89, 105
and physical maturity, 13, 40,
    41-5, 119-20
sex differences in, 40
see also cognitive development,
    mental ability
intestines, 21

jawbone, 22

knee, 12

language, 78, 80
larynx, 30, 138
learning, 68, 80, 81, 85, 125
perceptual, 84, 85
leg, 57-8
length, 23-4, 34
longitudinal studies, 16n., 18-19, 20,
    32, 67, 85, 86-7, 88, 100, 113
lungs, 27, 100
lymphoid tissue, 21, 23

malnutrition
and brain development, 70-1, 81
effects on growth, 100, 102-4,
    105-7, 108, 109, 121
see also nutrition, starvation
medulla, 69, 70, 138
memory, 68, 81-2
menarche
age variation in, 32-3, 95-6, 99,
    114, 119
and climate, 100, 119
and secular trend, 118, 119
and skeletal age, 36-7
mental
ability, 41-5, 66, 68, 79, 86, 89,
    107, 121, see also intelligence
development, see cognitive
    development
subnormality, 44, 60, 105, 107
midbrain, 69, 70, 71, 135
mongolism, 60
motor area of brain, 74, 76, 77, 79,
    135
movement control, 70-1, 76, 78

muscular
growth, 21, 23-4, 27, 110
strength, 24-5, 27
myelin, 73, 81, 138
myelination in brain, 74, 76n., 77-8,
    79, 81, 85-6, 138
myopia, 22-3, 138

National Child Development Study
    (UK), 44, 113, 114
neck, 76
nervous system, development of, 55,
    66, 67, 68, 80, 82, 84, see also
    brain, spinal cord
and education, 124-5
neuroglia, 72, 73, 138
neurons, 72-3, 74, 82-3, 85, 88,
    138-9
Nissl substance, 73, 74, 76
nutrition, 90, 91, 100, 102-10,
    111-12, 116, 121
normal requirements, 104-5
see also malnutrition, starvation

occipital lobe of brain, 74, 77, 82,
    138
oestrogen, 28, 29, see also hormones
ovaries, 27-8, 139

parent-child
correlations of growth, 54, 66,
    92-5
interaction, 60, 89
parietal lobe of brain, 77, 138
penis, 30-1, 56
personality, 47, 60, see also emotional
    development, psychological
    disturbances
pituitary
gland, 28-9, 56, 98, 137
hormones, 28-30
pons, 69, 70, 71, 139
premature babies, 81
psychological disturbances, 33, 46-7,
    48, 60, 111, 113
psychological functions, development
    of, 40, 60
puberty, precocious, 29, 40, 60

racial differences in growth, 98-100

reproductive organs, 21, 30-3
  development of, 30-3, 56
reticular formation, 78
retina, 55, 59, 77, 82-3, 139
rubella, 55

school-leaving age, 48-9, 123-4
seasonal effect on growth rate,
  100-2, 112
secular trend, 11, 13, 19-20, 104,
  115-20, 123
  data from countries, 115-16,
  117-18
sensitive period, 11, 13, 55-6, 68, 90,
  125
sensory area of brain, 74, 77, 85, 135
sex differences, 12, 23, 24-7, 54, 93
  in brain function?, 80, 81, 85
  in developmental age, 40
  in velocity of growth, 18, 32, 57-8,
  81
skeletal
  age, 35-40, 53, 63, 64, 95, 121
  growth, 21, 22, 23, 27, 42, 104,
  108, 109
  see also bones
skull, 21, 22, 59, 92
social deprivation
  and intellectual development, 109
  and physical growth, 105-6, 110,
  121
socio-economic class
  and intelligence, 44, 45, 107
  and physical growth, 44, 45, 105,
  113-14, 115
spatial ability, 80
spinal cord, 69-70, 71, 72, 74, 76
  83, 136

starvation, 13, 29, 51-2, see also
  malnutrition, nutrition
  in utero, 54, 70, 105, 106-7, 109
sterility, 56
subcutaneous fat, 21, 23, 24, 91
  measurements of, 23, 24

teeth, 36, 38-40, 42, 86
  eruption of, 36, 40, 95-6
  and skeletal age, 38, 39, 42
  see also dental age
temporal lobe of brain, 74, 77, 138
testes, 27-8, 30, 56, 139
testosterone, 28, 56, see also hormones
thalamus, 69, 140
thigh, 25, 57
thyroid
  gland, 30, 39
  hormone, 30, 39, 54, 81
toes, 59
tonsils, 21, 23
trunk, 23, 24, 58
twins, 50, 65, 81, 92, 95, 100-1, 110

variability, of growth, 12, 14, 16, 20,
  30-3, 34, 81, 86, 95-7, 100-1,
  121-3, 125-6
vision, 59, 77, 78, 82-3
visual area of brain, 74, 76, 77

walking, development of, 40, 61-2,
  81, 86
weight, 68, 100, 104, 111, 113
  as measure of growth, 23, 30, 42,
  113
wrist, 35, 62, 74, 79, 81

X-ray, 16, 23, 35, 36, 38